COLD NOSES
at the
PEARLY GATES

COLD NOSES
at the
PEARLY GATES

A Book of Hope for Those Who Have Lost a Pet

GARY KURZ

CITADEL PRESS
Kensington Publishing Corp.
www.kensingtonbooks.com

CITADEL PRESS BOOKS are published by

Kensington Publishing Corp.
850 Third Avenue
New York, NY 10022

Previously published by the author.

All Kensington titles, imprints, and distributed lines are available at special quantity discounts for bulk purchases for sales promotions, premi-
ums, fund-raising, educational, or institutional use. Special book excerpts
or customized printings can also be created to fit specific needs. For
details, write or phone the office of the Kensington special sales manager:
Kensington Publishing Corp., 850 Third Avenue, New York, NY 10022,
attn: Special Sales Department; phone: 1-800-221-2647.

First Citadel printing: April 2008

30 29 28 27 26 25 24

Printed in the United States of America

Library of Congress Control Number: 2007937049

ISBN-13: 978-0-8065-2887-8
ISBN-10: 0-8065-2887-7

To my many pet friends who shared not only my home,
but my heart . . .
Tinkerbell, Scooter, Miko, Fuji, Samantha, and Pebbles.
You have all gone on ahead.
I will catch up to you later.

The years may seem to slowly pass
Memories may begin to wane
The time we long for will come at last
When we shall be together again

—Dad

Contents

Foreword

For centuries, perhaps millennia, the matter of animals having souls has been a neglected literary topic, and yet it is a subject that has been, and remains, dear to the hearts of an overwhelming majority of people. A few of yesteryear's theologians have made fleeting reference to the possibilities, both for and against, but none have actually provided a substantial thesis to support their opinions.

Suddenly, in the twenty-first century, there appears to be an avalanche of interest in whether animals have souls, in particular whether there is a providential plan for them beyond earthly existence. There seems to be no shortage of ideas on the subject, as myriad hypotheses are offered for public consumption. From Eastern philosophy to new age idealism, you can find books, magazines, e-zines, and websites that propagate just about any view you can imagine. Unfortunately, these include a substantial number that disallow any possibility that animals are eternal creatures.

Fortunately, when read, the reader quickly discovers these views to be flawed, because they are based on nothing more than opinion. Opinion without authoritative basis usually smacks of bias, and bias does not resonate well with rational, truth-seeking people. These opinions are sometimes amusing diversions, but cannot be taken seriously. At best they are unsupportable, flash-in-the-pan ideas destined for obscurity. People who are looking for hope and comfort over the loss of a precious pet are not satisfied by these whimsical views.

Especially egregious are the websites that erroneously use scripture to justify and support the imaginations of the people behind them. Even a cursory review of the scripture used on these websites reveals an absence of appropriate exegesis. Most passages are either taken out of context or assigned biased meanings that fit the philosophy of the writer rather than the intent of scripture.

Lack of credibility aside, however, there is another issue to consider. Why would anyone go to such lengths to publish their beliefs if they knew it would cause others emotional distress? Even if what they believe is true (and it isn't), what possible good could come from disseminating that information to others?

When I reflect on the reason God left His written Word for us, words like *build up* and *edify*, and terms like *comfort one another with these words* come to mind. An attempt to add more pain to people who are already grieving is almost incomprehensible to me and not at all in keeping with our charge to *love thy neighbor as thyself*. When Jesus saw the people weeping at the grave of Lazarus, we are told that he too wept. He felt the grief of those mourning and sympathized with them. He had compassion for them.

This, then, is the example people who claim to know him must follow. When they quote the Bible, it should be to lift up and encourage, not tear down and defeat. Jude 22 says, *"and of some having compassion, making the difference."* The purpose of the Bible is to encourage mankind to reconcile with God and to enrich the individual with the truths it contains.

Without doubt there are times when the message from scripture is blunt and should be expressed as a warning. However, even in these instances, the call of God is *"Come unto me all ye that are heavy laden and I will give you rest"* (Matthew 11:28). It is soothing, not seething.

There is no basis for publishing a negative message on this subject of animal afterlife. There is no reason to purposely and maliciously cause those in pain to suffer more. The reckless and callous flavor of such behavior causes me to suspect that a need to further one's bias is behind these efforts rather than a desire to educate and edify.

In *Cold Noses at the Pearly Gates*, indisputable and convincing evidence is offered to prove that God has indeed made eternal provision for all of His creatures. God's providence and immutability are discussed in detail to show how they work together in relation to God's creation. Concepts and conclusions are based on reasonable interpretations of the entire text and not based on opinion. On those rare occasions where opinion is offered, it is appropriately identified as such.

COLD NOSES
at the
PEARLY GATES

INTRODUCTION

Who can one turn to when the unexpected suddenly happens and their precious pet is no more? Where can these people go for help? Often, these things happen without warning and so abruptly that there isn't even time to say good-bye to our wonderful best friends. Even if death is expected, it is still crushing and seems so final. It is as if we are in a bad dream that we cannot awaken from.

There are those learned professionals who stand ready to help us with our trauma and emotions. They are able to assist us to that place of acceptance, and help strengthen our resolve to recover from the blow. But they cannot mend the broken heart or fill the empty void left in our lives by the irreversible loss.

There is a balm for our hearts, however, a way to turn that emptiness into hope . . . a hope of seeing our pets again. As extraordinary as that may sound, I assure you that it is true. I regret that the circumstances that brought you to this book have occurred in your life, but I am confident that you will find a new

1

joy and hope from the literary journey on which you are about to embark.

A source of comfort is available that is higher than that offered by the many psychology books on the market today. There is a level of hope and anticipation that most people know absolutely nothing about and my desire is to make you aware of that hope.

In no way do I mean to lessen the worth of the many books that deal with the psychological and emotional recovery process following the loss of a pet. Quite the contrary. A psychology major myself at one point in my education, I found many of these works to be right on the mark and very helpful.

Indeed, these medical professionals understand the inner workings of our hearts and minds and what it takes to hasten the healing process. Their recovery advice is nothing less than excellent. Time is the great healer, but I believe some of their tips and ideas for rebounding actually speed up the healing process. I would suggest, therefore, that anyone who has suffered loss, pet or otherwise, acquire and use one of these books. It will help frame your feelings in a context that will allow you to understand what you are going through and why.

If I find any shortcomings at all in their writings, it would be that:

🐾 Irrespective of the great number of books available, I cannot recommend one more than the other. They are essentially clones of each other, and while all are good, none are better or worse than the other; and

🐾 While they are very helpful to the individual dealing with grief, they can only offer limited relief. Their final analysis appears to be "get over it and move on," which is not what most pet owners want to hear.

From a secular point of view, this advice of "closure" makes sense. It is the best natural conclusion that worldly knowledge can offer in regards to loss. This just is not enough for me. I know I have to get on with my life, and I am. But I really don't want to "get over it." I want to feel better. I want to stop hurting. But I certainly do not want to have closure in the sense some of these professionals intend.

Each of my departed pets left a permanent mark on my heart and a little more emptiness in my life. I love (please note the use of the present tense) each of them and I do not want to forget them at any level. I don't appreciate someone suggesting that I should. Most pet lovers would agree that this is just not an option. We no more want to think "that's it" for them, than we want to believe "that's it" for ourselves when we pass from this world.

As a student of the Bible and a disciple of the Lord Jesus Christ, I know better than to trust secular wisdom and understanding. There is higher wisdom, higher understanding, and higher help available. Where these other authors leave off, we will go on. Where natural understanding ends, we will seek the supernatural. We will find spiritual help to soothe both heart and spirit, to find real and lasting comfort to help in this time of need.

No matter what your spiritual beliefs or religious affiliation (or you may not even have or want any), if you are reading this

book because you have lost a beloved pet, you are probably dealing with the nagging questions that haunt most of us during these
awful times.

> *When our children ask these questions,*
> *we respond quickly with "Spot went to*
> *doggy heaven."*

You want to know if you will ever see your best friend again.
You want to know if there is more to life than just this earthly
existence. You want to know if there really is a God and if He
cares. You want to know, but you are afraid or ashamed to ask,
because until now no one was willing or able to answer you.

When our children ask these questions, we respond quickly
with "Spot went to doggy heaven," but we know that we have
no proof. We have no basis for what we tell our children except
we know that is what they need to hear. Inside we wish we had
a more convincing answer for them. Indeed, we wish we had an
answer for ourselves because our own breaking hearts yearn for
consolation.

It is at that point in our grieving that the psychologist can no
longer help and must take flight. It is here that their wise coun-
sel and books can no longer guide. It is here that someone with
genuine knowledge of the spiritual must rise to assist. It is for
this reason and this reason alone that this book was prepared.

If you are anything like me, you do not want closure. You want
comfort and hope and answers you can depend upon. You want

to know with certainty what has become of your best friend. I know of only one place to find supernatural comfort and hope that is dependable . . . the blessed Word of God.

That is exactly where this writer went to find true peace in my hour of need. My need was met, abundantly and totally, as God opened up my understanding of things I had not seen in his word before.

I think it is expedient for you to understand that I did not enter into this research as a novice. In fact, I have been a student of the Bible for more than thirty years with many years of accredited Bible courses and more than 22,000 hours of personal study in the sixty-six books that comprise the Old and New Testaments. Moreover, I have taught adult Sunday school and Bible studies for more than twenty-five years. It is important to my credibility that you know that I am very well acquainted with acceptable Bible research principles and appropriate exegesis of text.

Despite my education and experience, I feel I need to offer a disclaimer. It seems that no matter how many years one may study, no matter how familiar one may become with the Bible, there is always something new and great to learn from this blessed book. Periodically, circumstances too complex or overwhelming for us to handle come into our lives that remind us just how small we are and how little we know. It is then that we discover the very deep things of God in His word.

I may have read over a passage a hundred times before, but never saw the gem of knowledge it contained on another subject. Often I find that providential guidance does not come until the time I actually need it. It is as if "someone" was watching and knew. We will not visit in this study the question of whether that is by coincidence or design, but if you have been there, you could never subscribe to the former.

Such was the case with my studies for this work. I had a desperate need for comfort, and when I sought help and consolation from God's wonderful book, despite the fact that I had read the applicable verses so many times, a whole new understanding about animals was opened to me. Previous to my need, I had neither noticed nor considered what scripture had to say about animals. It simply never occurred to me to consider what became of them when they passed.

Our children are grown and on their own and our pets have become like children to us.

Motivated by need, I thoroughly researched the subject and now have full assurance of what the Bible teaches about animals. I now know that God has made provision for our pets and that we shall see them again. I may not get to feel their cold noses at the pearly gates as the title suggests, but there is no doubt in my mind that they will be there and that a grand reunion is only delayed by the passing of time.

When one of my closest pets passed unexpectedly, it hit my wife and me extremely hard. Our children are grown and on their own and our pets have become like children to us. To lose one to age is upsetting enough. As hard as that is to accept, you are somewhat readied for the eventuality because you know that age eventually takes us all.

To lose one prematurely, however, as was the case with our Chihuahua, Pebbles, is absolutely devastating. What's more, to live with the knowledge that it didn't have to happen at all is almost completely insurmountable.

Pebbles was a beautiful dog with tan and fawn colors. We had not been able to have her spayed as a puppy, but after testing Pebbles, the veterinarian ascertained that she could be spayed successfully at age seven with virtually no risk to her health.

I was very apprehensive about the procedure because of her age and weight (she was not obese, but very well padded at thirteen pounds—we had given her the nickname of "Garganchihuahua"). But the doctor assured us that it was a simple procedure and she was medically able to endure it.

His attempt to comfort us by saying "The operation went perfectly, she should have been okay" did little to alleviate the crushing pain we felt when he phoned with the unexpected bad news that she had passed. His comments a few minutes later when we arrived on the scene that "this had never happened before" also was little comfort.

Needless to say, my wife and I have punished ourselves over and over again for opting for the surgery. Pebbles really did not need to have it, but to eliminate the possibility of other health problems it seemed the safest thing to do. The surgery was more of a safeguard for her than a convenience for us. How we wish we had the opportunity to rethink that decision. How I wish I had listened to the little voice of apprehension inside.

You do not have to go through something like this (and I hope you never do) to understand what we were going through. A terrible void of loss and guilt prevailed in our home for the next several months. For weeks all my wife and I could do was drag ourselves to work, make it through the day, and then come home and just lay in bed weeping and comforting each other.

I wrote a lot of poetry and sulky prayers. The words just seemed to pour out of my heart. I think it is human nature to do such things when our hearts are broken. Somehow, writing something down helps to make us feel better. At one point I even thought to write a book on what it was like to endure a broken heart, but it was too hurtful to do so. It pleases me to author a more optimistic and uplifting book like this instead.

I wish I could accept full credit for coming up with the idea to research this subject. It would be quite an ego booster to know I was that spontaneous and creative. Unfortunately, my need, not my creativity, deserves the spotlight. The truth is, some credit belongs to someone else altogether. Oddly, the catalyst for motivating me was the lack of compassion of someone I counted as a friend.

One evening at church, shortly after losing Pebbles, she asked, "Why are you looking so glum, Gary"? I recounted the tragedy for her with tears in my eyes and a lump in my throat. Without so much as a sympathetic twinkle in her eye, she coldly, almost laughingly, responded with, "Oh and I suppose you think that she went to doggy heaven, don't you?" The implication was clear. She did not think so.

That curt, unfeeling reply cut deep. I hadn't expected it. It was like stepping into the path of an oncoming car that I didn't see coming. Her rudeness only served to deepen my sorrow and make me feel even more alone and helpless than I already felt. I don't know how I mustered the wherewithal to not strike back at her verbally, but somehow I did. I even managed a sickening chuckle to brush the conversation away, as most of us do in uncomfortable situations.

I confess that I was tempted to lash back at her for her insensitivity. I just did not feel like hurting her back and I was in no mood for conflict. Besides, there was an up side to this awful encounter. She unintentionally had made me face the question that I was hiding in my heart, the question I had been afraid to face. The same question many of you are hiding.

Now, there it was. It was out in the open. It had been uttered out loud. Where indeed did I think my precious Pebbles was? What was my position on this? Many people hold me as their mentor in the Bible . . . and I simply did not have an answer. I just didn't know. But I felt more than inept and insecure, I felt challenged. I wanted to know. And I was going to find out.

And find out I did! The Bible is full of guidance on this topic. And since I feel so certain that others want to know, too, I decided to record my research and pass it along. You will have to weigh my thoughts according to your own faith and convictions, but I hope you find the comfort and hope that I found.

Chapter 1
FACT, FAITH, AND FINDINGS

There is so much knowledge available in this world today. Students without access to a computer during the school day are quickly becoming the exceptions. They now have the world at their fingertips, and while they may not possess any more common sense than other generations did at their age, they certainly have absorbed more information and mastered the tools of our technological world.

I am told that computers, or at least certain computer groups, hold an estimated twenty to thirty pages of data on every person in the civilized world. Network news sources have estimated that the World Wide Web grows by more than 170,000 web pages every day, or over a million each week. That is amazing. At that rate, if a thousand people read one web page every ten minutes, non-stop, twenty-four hours a day, seven days a week, for the rest of their lives, they would lose ground and never catch up. Whew!

Technology is racing ahead of us at a blinding clip. Super computers now process billions of transactions in mere seconds. It boggles one's imagination. I admit it is becoming too much for me. As I sit in front of my multifunctional, multicolored, multimedia, voice-command computer, I am in complete awe of technology. I get headaches wondering how the programs on the tiny chips actually work. I wonder how anyone acquires the knowledge that enables them to put a computer together.

I also wonder what the future holds. My generation mockingly laughed at the 1960s Zager and Evans song "In the Year 2525," when it suggested that machines would be doing everything for us and that our arms and legs would hang at our side with nothing to do. Of course, there were no PCs back then, so it was just a song. Now, I wonder. I can open programs on my PC with voice commands without touching a key. Someday soon we will be able to operate everything we do on the machine simply by talking to it. And to think that thirty years ago the calculator was the discovery of the ages!

There are so many places we may go in order to gather information . . . the library, periodicals, files, and of course, computers. We can form opinions on virtually any subject, including technical subjects that are completely unfamiliar to us. We do not have to be experts, because the expert is now on the video or in the box on an electronic circuit board. We can acquaint ourselves with literally any aspect of any subject and become immediate novices through this blitz of information now available to us.

If we want to become experts, however, we must leave off from general knowledge writings and refer to the technical manual. General knowledge is usually some fact mingled with a lot of opinion. That is not a condemnation, just an observation. If we want to construct a boat, we need to follow technical blueprints that give us facts. If we want to build a gas turbine, that, too, requires technical expertise and facts that can only be obtained from the accepted technical manuals.

The same is true of this topic of life after death after life. Literally tons of nontechnical reference materials exist on this subject, written by all sorts of people with all types of credentials—and motives. These people give you some fact and a lot of opinion. These facts are not technical, but qualify rather as general, basic knowledge. If we want expert fact and guidance on this topic, we must go to the technical manual. The technical manual on life and death is, in my opinion, the Holy Bible. In this matter of animal afterlife, use of the Bible becomes so much more important because there is a lack of general knowledge available to help form an opinion.

It is here, in the Bible, where we learn of mankind's (meaning men and women from the Greek word *Cosmos*) beginning, end, and eternity. Many individuals scoff at the Bible, but the fact is this book alone has an authority unknown to the sum total of all other books written by men and women, including this very one that you are reading.

Nevertheless, many have put that self-proclaiming truth aside and undertaken, with nothing but their own opinion as a basis, to produce writings that are in conflict with the Bible. These writings do not diminish the unimpeachable authority of the Bible, nor detract from the account of mankind it contains.

I do not wish to offend anyone with my position on the Bible. I merely want to establish from the outset that I revere the Bible above any other writing and that the Bible is the technical manual that I consulted and yielded to in all of the conclusions drawn herein. Where better could someone turn to learn about the here-after, than to the timeless, yet timely book that was authored by the one who lives there?

I think a quote from this great book will underscore why I rely on the Bible so totally for comfort and guidance. I know the quote is taken a bit out of the context for which it was given, but the tenet of comforting others that it sets forth is prevalent throughout scripture. Simply, it reads:

> *Wherefore, comfort one another with these words.*
> **—I Thessalonians 4:18**

These words were penned by the Apostle Paul and delivered to the church at Thessalonica. They were intended to be thoughts of encouragement and comfort, not only for the folks in that time, but for any and all who would place their trust in God the Son. His words teach us a valuable principle that I would like to address. To do so, we must first understand the circumstances that prompted his being directed to write to this church. This may take us on a short rabbit trail, but I assure you, it is important to the case I am building.

The faith of the Thessalonians was wavering. They were making the classic spiritual mistake that most believers make at one time or another in their Christian experience . . . they were "thinking" instead of "believing." Faith is the "substance of things hoped for, the evidence of things not seen" (Hebrews 11:1)—or, in other words, faith is believing God. Doubt was starting to take hold. The Thessalonians were wondering what had become of their departed loved ones. Paul assured them through these inspired passages that they would meet their dead in Christ again. What a marvelous comfort this must have been—to have such a giant in the faith confirm the promise of God to them.

> *If you are taking time to read this book, it is likely that you are doing so because you have recently had the misfortune of losing a pet.*

Now, before you raise a wary doctrinal eyebrow, let me assure you that I am not trying to include animals in the event that is addressed in this portion of scripture, an event endearingly known to those of the Christian faith as the "rapture." Rather, I am illustrating the attribute of God to exercise providential care over the grieving and to give them comfort and hope as He did here through the Apostle Paul. His word is full of examples of his caring and loving nature. The principle is clear . . . we are to "comfort one another" in spiritual matters. It is in obedience to this command that I offer my thoughts and conclusions on the many issues associated with what happens when our loving pets come to the end of their earthly road.

If you are taking time to read this book, it is likely that you are doing so because you have recently had the misfortune of losing a pet, or perhaps are concerned that you someday will have to face that eventuality. Since our life spans are so much longer than that of the animals we take as pets, unless you are very old and yourself at risk of expiring, the chances are very good that your concerns are justified.

A dear friend of mine—Will—is one of the most kindhearted people I have ever met. He asked me rhetorically one morning in regards to his three-year-old dog named Sweetheart, "Gary, what will I ever do if she dies?" Will and his wife had no children. They were wrapped up totally in their little girl Sweetheart. I know Will loved her deeply, like a child, because she was spoiled just like someone spoils a child. He once brought her to my office to introduce her to me. She promptly squatted and soiled my carpet. All Will could manage through his ear-to-ear grin was "Isn't she precious!"

Then Will asked me a question that he obviously wanted an answer to. He said, "Gary, do pets go to heaven?" He knew I was a Baptist preacher and that I knew the Bible well. He expected an answer, and I wish I could have given him one, but the truth was, I just did not know.

The question, therefore, went unanswered. Now, a dozen years later, as I bring my work and research to paper, Will and Sweetheart come to mind. If Sweetheart is still alive, she would be nearly sixteen. I know Will is still alive because once a year or so we exchange cards or e-mail. So one of the first copies of this book will be heading to my good friend. I am happy that I will finally be able to answer his question. I know he will rejoice to know that he will see his Sweetheart again.

If you are anything like Will or me, then I suspect your motive for reading this book is to find answers, to find comfort for the loss you feel. If that is so, coincidentally, your reason for reading this book parallels my motive for writing it. I simply was seeking comfort for the pain of losing a very special and very close friend.

One could misconstrue this book's contents then as nothing more than wishful thinking, and that I was grasping for anything to bring my grieving heart relief. While I have no doubt that my grief moved me to seek answers and help from the scriptures, I assure you that I was dreadfully aware of the danger of allowing my heart to make the Bible say what I wanted it to say, and I guarded myself diligently from being so swayed.

My grief did not cause me to abandon the fundamental principles of research. I know all too well how people fool themselves into applying what they want to be true to what is actually true, and I did not want to fall into that trap. I do not mean that people are intentionally deceitful, but rather that they allow emotions to sway them into massaging what is said into what they want to hear.

I simply love the Bible, and I love learning new things from it. I began seeing things about animals that I had never seen before.

I assure you that I did not build and document a self-serving case. I will admit that had my research led me to conclude that animals have no part in the afterlife, I probably would not have written a book on the subject. That conclusion would have been too depressing to do so. Nevertheless, if the Bible did teach that, I would have accepted it as truth and somehow managed to cope with that awful revelation. Thank God this was not the case; it is clear that He loves these creatures and finds great pleasure in them.

Actually, while grief served as the ignition to get me started in my research, it did not remain my motivator for long. Somewhere early on in my research, during prayer and meditation, my grief took a backseat to enthusiasm. I simply love the Bible, and I love learning new things from it. I began seeing things about animals that I had never seen before. It absolutely staggered me that I had spent so much time in the Bible and had never paid attention to this subject.

As a result of this discovery, I have spent thousands of hours studying and learning and have come up with many exciting conclusions and ideas that I want to share with you. I have tried to capture each of my observations as clearly and honestly as possible.

I must confess that there is not an abundance of scripture that addresses the eternity of animals, which may explain the virtual absence of books on the subject throughout the ages. Still, God gives us a wealth of passages associated with animals and how important they are.

While the exact topic of animal afterlife is not specifically addressed in detail, I want you to understand that there are many other subjects not addressed directly in the Bible, for which we humans lack no opinion. People take stands on all sorts of things, often claiming a biblical origin, when in fact, there is no specific guidance.

How do we arrive at these spiritual positions? Simply, we use the tools God has provided to each of us. We look at applicable passages, evaluate other, related principles found in other passages, consider all the associated nonbiblical information, and apply deductive reasoning (logic).

Let me give an example of how these tools work together to give us discernment on a particular subject. Consider the subject of illegal drugs. Is there anyone in the civilized world today who is not enlightened about the ill effects of natural or synthetic chemicals upon the human body? I should think not. Even those who are enslaved by these habit-forming drugs and who continue to punish their bodies day after day with them readily admit that they wish they could free themselves from the suffering it causes them.

Now then, the Bible mentions drugs in several places, none which really could be applied to prove overwhelmingly that drugs are harmful. The Bible does not say, "Thou shalt not use cocaine," for instance. We have no clear teaching on that particular drug. We know it hurts our bodies. We know it is illegal to possess and use. But hey, the Bible doesn't specifically mention cocaine, so. . . .

We are told to "rightly divide the truth" by the Bible. In other words, we are to let it interpret itself. By comparing scripture to scripture, we can arrive at constants or truths. To conclude cocaine is okay by the Bible is to wrongfully divide the word of truth. If we know it is harmful and sometimes fatal to our bodies, we know the Bible teaches an associated principle that precludes the use of cocaine. The Bible teaches we should care for our bodies as a temple. Applying logic tells us not only that cocaine is not good, but that it is in fact, bad.

There is no clear guidance, but building upon principles from the word and applying logic, we arrive at a conclusion, a very solid one at that. Similarly, when it comes to our beloved pets, there is no clear guidance that says "animals go to heaven." However, we can use the same tools we used in our example to arrive at a supportable position on this topic.

Obviously I cannot assure you that all the conclusions in this book are ironclad, right on the mark, exactly as I tell you facts. I believe them to be, but I am only a man. I labored hard to arrive at the conclusions here. I would not mislead, nor would I ever present something as fact if I were not convinced it were so.

But, to be fair, this is new ground we are covering. To my knowledge, no one has ever attempted to research, catalog, and expound upon this topic from a biblical perspective before. I received virtually no help in my research and spent many long, tiring hours on this project. Consequently, the potential for error in some of my "ideas" exists. Someone, perhaps you, may come along and say "Hey, good job, but did you consider this!" I welcome your constructive input. You might enhance this work and have a hand in helping someone in need. That is how technical works are refined.

Having said all that, the bottom line for me is that I feel very confident that the conclusions I present in this book are a factual, close representation. Embodied in my confidence, however, beyond the research, is my faith in God and His goodwill toward His creation. That faith was a critical factor in my research and therefore contributed greatly to the development of my conclusions. As a consequence, while I know my conclusions to be true and am able to transfer that knowledge to you, I cannot transfer my faith. That is something you will have to provide.

Chapter 2

CREATURE OR CREATION

THEIR BIG DAY

There are any number of views of how, when, and where animals originated. Some are religious or faith based. Others are not. Largely, they are all in contrast with each other. It is not my intention to agitate anyone, but I do need to discuss the most popular views on this topic because my position will serve as one of the foundational footers for this chapter, and perhaps the entire book. I realize that people in all the major camps of thinking are equally passionate about their views. If your view is somewhat in contrast with mine, I hope you will understand how my passion drives me to hold the convictions that I do.

The three most popular views are evolution, theistic evolution (more currently referred to as "Superior Design"), and creation. There certainly are others, but in our Western culture, these are the top three. I will give a brief overview of each in the following pages.

Predictably, I sit in the camp of creationism. I am a Christian and my faith hinges on the authority of the Bible. If I am to believe at all, I must believe it all. How anyone can believe part of the Bible and disbelieve another part is beyond my comprehension. If we were wise enough to discern what is inerrant and what is not, we would have no need for the Bible at all (for the record, I believe it all to be). That notwithstanding, the Bible teaches that animals were created and I accept that. If you do not share all of my convictions concerning creation, that is fine. Please continue reading. The goal of this book is to comfort you, not to convert you to my way of thinking.

> *The goal of this book is to comfort you, not to convert you to my way of thinking.*

On the other hand, if you totally reject creationism and/or the Bible or God, I honestly believe you will most certainly not enjoy this book. Belief in God and scripture is foundational to many of the concepts and conclusions I discuss. I do not wish to mislead anyone. This is why I ensured the title clearly suggested that the book was Christian in persuasion (i.e., "Pearly Gates").

I feel compelled to point out before I define each of the three teachings, that if I were writing this book 200 years ago, this chapter would not be necessary. This is because 200 years ago there would have been only one position to discuss . . . creationism. The other two major philosophies are virtual newcomers, whose origins (forgive the pun on evolution) are somewhat presumptuous and untrustworthy, to say the least.

Now then, let us move on to the overview of the three major

views of how life, and therefore animals, began. I will list them in reverse popularity order. This is not my opinion, but the statistical result of conducted polls.

First up, the least popular view.

Evolution

I have read much of Darwin's work, and the works of several of his successors, or rather, supporters. I consider these men and women sincere in their beliefs, but I do not consider them correct. Many of the proponents of evolution expect their assumptions to be accepted by the general public without the scientific validation and ratification that they claim the Christian faith lacks.

Faith neither claims nor needs scientific validation; although there is overwhelming scientific evidence to support the claims of the Bible. For true Christians, faith is the evidence of things not seen. It is taking God at His word and believing Him, and requires no physical proof.

Despite the inability of so-called science to validate the claims of evolution, that is not my primary problem with this view. What bothers me most about evolutionary evidence is that it hinges more on faith than faith does. Let me explain. If you have read any of the dissertations that generate from this group of people, especially from papa Darwin himself, you cannot help but notice that there is a commonality present and prevalent in their writings. In everything I have read, assertions of fact are almost uniformly preceded by qualifiers such as "perhaps," "could be," "I think," or "maybe." Evolution, from my perspective, requires a whole lot more faith than does faith itself. And if I am going to put faith in a person, it is going to be the infinite person of the Lord and not a finite person much like myself.

The evolutionist basically excludes God from the equation altogether, and credits the persevering adaptability of the creature and nature's ability to select the strong and eliminate the weak as the reason for life and its progress in evolution. Evolutionists may say they still believe in God, but in the final analysis, they must deny Him in order to embrace their doctrine. If they come close to recognizing God at all, it would be in their attempt to personify Mother Nature or Mother Earth by giving credit to that perceived deity for all that happens in our world.

As tempting as it is to me to refute the assumptions of evolution, this is really not the time or place to do so. I have already said more than I had intended. To say more would serve no purpose other than to dominate the available time and space and further irritate those who do not share my views on evolution. It is sufficient to say that evolution not only eliminates God from the whole picture, but in so doing, precludes the existence of an afterlife for either man or beast . . . in other words, no need for God then, no need for God now, no need for God later.

Up next . . .

Theistic Evolution

This close kin of evolution is a relatively new position on the origin of life, one that has drawn much attention. It has lured away many from what were considered evolution and creation strongholds. It is difficult to say whether this view has overtaken evolution theory in popularity, but if it hasn't, it no doubt soon will. It is safe to say, however, that it has won converts from both evolution and creation circles.

Let me be as simple in defining this view so we do not confuse the two lines of thought. Theistic, from the root word *theo*, or "of or pertaining to God," when put together with the philosophy of evolution, suggests a blending of evolution and creation doctrine. In other words, God had a hand in provoking the evolutionary progress of the planet and all the species that populated it. Proponents of this position contend that we can now accept the doctrinal claims of evolution because they do not infringe upon the teachings of the Bible about creation. Conversely, evolutionists can accept God and the account of creation because there is a viable meeting of the two teachings.

Here is how they manage this . . . they say that the "day" mentioned in the Bible is not a literal twenty-four-hour period. Instead, they assign an arbitrary number of years to each of the six days of creation, such as 1,000,000. In other words, each day in the Bible really represents 1 million years. I said the number was arbitrary, because some scientists do not subscribe to the 1 million year assignment, but chose rather 1 billion years.

It is interesting to note that the evolutionists can be so sure that God did not mean what He said, but they cannot even agree among themselves as to the measure of time. Regardless, the intent is obvious. They want to make evolution more acceptable to those who cannot stomach a straight shot of evolution. It is a compromised position to neutralize and win over opponents to evolution theory.

Besides finding this philosophy objectionable and unsupportable, I find this obvious ploy to "sneak" in the evolution idea under the cloak of theism in keeping with any misguided attempt to make the Bible support one's personal view.

Even the most cursory or elementary study of the Bible would show each day of creation to be a literal twenty-four-hour period. The scripture clearly states "the evening and the morning" were the first day. The same words are used in many different places in both the Old and the New Testaments, each time alluding to a twenty-four-hour period. Are we to interpret the Lord's request to his disciples to "watch until morning" to mean he wanted them to wait around for a million years? Of course not. But that is what we must believe if we change the measure of time assigned to the word day.

Do not expect supporters of the Theistic Evolution view to accept this explanation. To do so, they would be inclined to also acknowledge the authority of God's word over their own supposition. That is a very hard thing to do. It is much easier to correct what they see as an obvious error by God in the creation account.

I had not intended to refute anything about evolution, but I must offer this one scientific argument for your consideration. There are many other strong arguments, but this one is one of the hardest to ignore. If we look at Theistic Evolution with a purely scientific eye and apply literally the claim that is made by evolution, to wit: that each day represents a designated period of time (let's say 1 million years), and acknowledge that during this time natural selection and development of the existing species took place, then we run into a very big scientific problem.

Applying other accepted rules of science—for example, photosynthesis—we cannot reconcile the long periods of time assigned to each of the six creation days. In other words, if plants formed on one day (or over a period of 1 million years), animals during a subsequent million years, and the sun appeared after that, how did the species survive at all?

We know by scientific principles that plants cannot survive very long without sunlight. But according to some Theistic Evolutionists, they survived a million years without sunlight. Even more outrageous, a billion years according to others. It is simply amazing that these plants flourished in the dark for such a long period. But then, who can argue with science?

Theistic Evolution, then, is a hard pill to swallow, more difficult even than the theory of evolution itself.

We are not done yet. We still must reconcile the problematic theory that plants and animals existed so long without the mutual exchange of oxygen and carbon dioxide needed to supply each other. Science tells us that neither can live without the other for any extended time. But again, Theistic Evolutionists would have us believe they did just that for millions, perhaps billions, of years.

Just think about that period of time . . . millions, perhaps billions, of years. That is an extraordinarily long time to go without critical elements needed to sustain life. Think how very impossible that would be. Think of how long it takes to live our lives. What would our earth be like without the sun during our short lifetime? Take away the plants and the animals, too. It just would not work. You could not possibly survive. And we only live for about seventy years or so. Now imagine 13,000 generations of your descendants living under those conditions and surviving. And I only used 1 million years as our base. Most evolution "authorities" speak in terms of billions of years. Talk about needing faith to support what you believe!

The impact of such a drawn-out ecosystem would be quickly felt and life would die off as rapidly as it appeared. Plants could not live without the sun. Animals could not live without the plants. I am not saying that the entire chain of life would break down. I am saying it would never be established. Life could not exist under this imagined matrix.

Theistic Evolution, then, is a hard pill to swallow, more difficult even than the theory of evolution itself. Not only does it include most of the preposterous assumptions of evolution, but it becomes unscientific and self-defeating in its own doctrine.

Finally . . .

Creation

Some time back, perhaps tweny years ago, I recall reading some of Darwin's writings. I was not really curious about evolution, but I could hardly discuss or refute his views if I had never acquainted myself with them. As a Bible student, I immediately detected a difference in Darwin's writing from the estimated forty men used to write the books of the Bible. It was not convincing. It was even less than that. It was weak. His case was weak and the evidence he presented was questionable at best.

I could not put my finger on why there was such an over-whelming perception of insecurity in his writing. At first I thought it might just be his style of writing, but it was not. Then I discovered that it wasn't the author or the subject he wrote on that disagreed with me. It wasn't even the amazing jumps that were made to arrive at some of the conclusions he drew. What really bothered me was the lack of conviction and certainty with which he presented his so-called evidence.

After so many years, I am sure I cannot quote any portion of his work accurately, but I vividly recall an avalanche of disclaimers he used throughout his work. I remember counting several hundred times the use of the words and phrases *maybe*, *perhaps*, *I think*, and *it could be*. I admit, I do not know what was in this man's mind or heart, but as a writer I can affirm that a book usually projects the writer's thoughts and ideas. With this in mind, his use of such non-persuasive language suggests a lack of conviction. I have a hard time understanding how the philosophical descendents of Darwin can be so strong in their beliefs when Darwin himself appears not to have been.

Conversely, the account of creation is relayed to us via the best-selling and therefore, most popular book in history. It is housed in a book that has been used to successfully prove historical and archaeological fact, facts that scientists and historians often disputed, without basis or success. For instance, in the book of Daniel we are told that Nebuchadnezzar was once the king of Babylon. Historians balked at this account for many years. They assured us that not only had this man not been the king, he had never even been to the city of Babylon. Imagine their surprise when twentieth-century archaeologists uncovered the ruins of

Babylon and found that not only had Nebuchadnezzar been to Babylon, not only had he been the king of Babylon, but that every brick in the city had his name imprinted upon it.

Which is more palatable to the human heart and spirit: a book written by a finite man, that seems to lack conviction; or an infinite book written by an infinite God that has authoritatively found its way into the homes of countless masses? Without even addressing the supernatural uniqueness of the Bible, we must recognize its immeasurable worth in history, geography, culture, and social reform. Moreover, it is a book of unmatched authority and wisdom, with no instance, not even one hint of supposition or guesswork. Rather, it overwhelms its reader with certainty and authority and instills strong faith.

Creationists are so called because we accept a literal rendering of the creation account of Genesis, chapter 1, to wit: plants on the third day; sun, moon, and stars on the fourth; birds and fish on the fifth; and all other animals and mankind on the sixth— all days being a literal twenty-four-hour period of time. They all survived because they did not have to exist long alone, but almost immediately found themselves in a mutually supportive role.

Having removed any doubt as to my position on animal origin, let us move on to a discussion of the actual day of the creation of animals, their big day if you will. On day five, the fish and birds arrived. We will put them aside temporarily and address them collectively with all other animals later on. Let's move on to day six, the day when the animals that science calls "mammals" were created.

THEIR PURPOSE

It is at this point that we need to make a distinction as to what animals we are primarily concerned with in this matter of afterlife. Let me say first that I feel certain that God has a plan and place for all the creatures He has created. Chapter 4 addresses this subject in greater depth. The singular thrust of this book, however, is to give comfort to those who have lost animals they love. I understand that this opens up a wide range of animals. It could include wild animals that we have befriended, domestic beasts of burden or farm animals that we grew up with, but we are primarily speaking of those animals that come from that group of wonderful creatures we have come to call "pets."

From this point forward, therefore, I will use the term *pets* and *animals* almost interchangeably, but my thoughts will lean more toward domesticated animals, especially those we allow to live among us in and around our homes. In no way does that exclude the others, but let us concern ourselves with those who capture our hearts and share our lives.

No doubt, the closeness that animals and humans enjoyed allowed Adam an insight we no longer enjoy today.

I think it is important to note that wild or undomesticated animals did not always exist. In fact, domesticated beasts of burden did not always exist, either. There were no wild animals in the beginning. There were no plow horses or working oxen. All animals were tame, given the role of companion to mankind, and both dwelled together in peace and harmony.

In fact, the harmony was so profound, God tasked Adam with naming each animal at his discretion. I think we have all wondered where Adam came up with some of the names he assigned. Whatever gave him the idea for aardvark or platypus? Why ostrich or orangutan? No doubt, the closeness that animals and humans enjoyed allowed Adam an insight we no longer enjoy today. It is difficult to second-guess him now.

In light of all this, it is not a stretch of either truth or imagination to assume that all animals originally existed in a "pet" status. It is convincingly apparent that this was precisely the role God had intended for them. We can safely conclude then (and please if you get nothing else from this book, be sure to grasp these key points) that God:

🐾 Knew what He wanted to do in regard to creation

🐾 Had the power to bring His plan to pass

🐾 Created a perfect environment

🐾 Created man in a perfect state of spirit, mind, and body

🐾 Created perfect animals to share perfect mankind's perfect domain

🐾 Intended for this perfect situation to continue forever, without death for either human or animal

When he had completed his act of creation, we are told that God surveyed his perfect work and gave us this assessment of what He had made:

And God saw everything that he had made, and
behold, it was very good.
—Genesis 1:31

He was extremely happy with His work and with the relationship he had orchestrated between mankind and animals. Lest we forget who we are talking about here, it was GOD who did the work and GOD who made the assessment. We aren't talking about "the man upstairs" or "the big guy," irreverent terms I have come to detest. We are talking about GOD, who alone has power to create and take life. He created, and He created perfectly. And He was very pleased with what He had created.

The fact that this perfect situation would eventually change is not because God created us with a flaw, but rather because we exercised our free will to bring imperfection into our lives. As a result of man's tragic fall away from God through disobedience (discussed in greater detail later), our animal friends were also changed and we now have wild beasts and beasts of burden.

Animals now fear man. I cannot say that I blame them after what we did to their perfect world. Still, our relationship with them was not totally lost. From the ruins of our original relationship came a group of animals we simply refer to now as "pets."

Another result of the fall of mankind manifested itself in the plant world. Previously, man and animal consumed fruits, grains, and vegetables. Neither man nor beast labored as they co-existed in peaceful harmony, eating the abundant fruit and vegetation. Food was plentiful. Now, after the fall, flora did not grow as plentiful as before. Now people were forced to till the ground and toil to obtain it.

Man now hunted for and consumed meat to offset the diminished vegetation. He had to work to survive. His load was heavy. He learned to depend upon domesticated beasts to help him do his work. He fed the beasts in return. The harmonious co-existence was now more of a co-dependence. To this day, even though our pets still serve in the role of companion, they also are, to varying degrees, beasts of burden, serving as K9 police, sled dogs, mousers on farms, and so forth. Some people even breed or show their pets to supplement their incomes.

Despite that, the lion's share (I couldn't resist using an animal cliché) of pets are loved and cherished as companion animals. In truth, the relationship is still one of mutual dependency. Pets give us love and devotion. They greet us after work and make us feel special. We in turn give back love and provision and make them feel special. It is an age-old relationship, dating back further than anyone can remember or research. As long as there have been people and animals, there has been a relationship between the two. And what a grand relationship it has been, transcending every ethnic and cultural border, in every climate or topographical setting, at sea, in space, on the frozen tundra or in the dry desert, in peace or war. Throughout every age, pets have been by our side as an intricate part of our world and history.

You can find images of pets painted on the walls of caves, captured in medieval sculpture, and immortalized on canvas. Presidents have brought them fame. Cities have erected their statues. In a thousand ways, as long as mankind has existed, we have paid tribute to these wonderful creatures that have walked by our side.

Their unreserved loyalty and dedication have generated a wealth of written testimonials. For those of you who have computers, I urge you to search any number of websites under the keywords "Pet Loss." On one hand these places are sad to visit, perhaps one of the saddest on earth, because literally thousands of good-bye notes and stories about pets can be found. However, there is also an air of honor and nobleness present as we read of champions and fathom the impact they had upon the lives of their humans. [I spend a lot of time reading these accounts. I could never post my own as I am just not that strong. I keep my pain private. This book is a major step for me, sharing a very personal part of my life with others.]

There is no doubt but that these wonderful furry and feathered best friends are an intricate part of who we are and what we are about. I recall many years ago one of the most endearing testimonials to this. While on active duty in the U.S. Coast Guard, stationed at home in Hawaii, an electronic message (not e-mail, but a radio-transmitted signal) came across the wire. The message was for all Coast Guard personnel in the entire district, which basically included the entire South Pacific. It seems Shackles, the mascot dog on one of our Loran stations on a tiny atoll, had passed away of old age.

Hundreds, if not thousands, of sailors had stroked that dog's fur over the years. Shackles had provided companionship to many lonely souls stationed at that isolated outpost, so many miles from home. Many a sailor had found him a faithful substitute for family and friends. He lifted their spirits and made home seem a little closer for them.

When he passed, the hearts of those who were currently sta-

Our history is peppered with accounts of great animals and the great help and service they have been to us.

tioned with him were broken and they felt compelled to send a message out to other sailors in the Pacific basin who may have known this fine friend.

To understand the significance of this act, you need to know that this sort of message is strictly taboo over official military communication nets. Infractions are not tolerated and disciplinary action is usually swift and sure. Despite the rules, not one complaint was registered by any of the thousands of user installations. In fact, the message was received and passed on from command to command until almost every unit in the Coast Guard had received word. If you didn't know Shackles, you knew of him. He was a sailor. He was a shipmate. He served his country well until he could serve no more. And then he was given a sailor's farewell.

Our history is peppered with accounts of great animals and the great help and service they have been to us. Their tales touch us deeply and dearly. There are a million stories, but I think sharing a few would be an appropriate way to honor them collectively. It might also serve to cheer up the grieving and maybe soften the hearts of those readers not yet convinced of the eternal importance of these wonderful creatures.

I will not cheapen my attempt to magnify our animal friends by alluding to stories of Lassie, Rin Tin Tin, or Morris the cat. While these were all intelligent and entertaining characters, they

were nothing more than actors in our living rooms and the stories they played out were the concoctions of Hollywood writers.
I have no doubt but that each of them were great pets to someone, but they were just animal thespians to the rest of us, champions of the make-believe. I chose rather to recount a few stories
about real life, touching episodes of almost unbelievable determination, achievement, and dedication . . . to show that animals
have had and continue to have important roles in this world and
the next.

Almost immediately, one story comes to mind that appeared
in a Honolulu newspaper more than two decades ago. It seems
an Australian rancher was taking a break from the hot sun. He
had walked to a nice little bluff overhanging a lake and had stripped
down to his unmentionables to take a dip. As he made his way
to the edge of the bluff, intending to dive in, his herding dog
jumped in front of him and began to growl.

The rancher was startled. The dog had never acted like this
before. He was a kindhearted dog who got along with all the other
animals and people on the farm. It was so unlike him to display
such a mean temper. The rancher shouted, "Get out of the way
dawg," and started again to the edge of the bluff. The dog again
blocked his path, this time showing his teeth and growling even
more viciously than the first time. The rancher, wondering if his
dog had gone mad, again scolded the dog, saying, "What is wrong
with you, dawg, get on out of the way," while making a sweep-
ing motion with his foot.

Apparently seeing that he was not going to stop his master
from going to the bluff, the dog turned and ran off the edge of
the bluff himself, falling the five or six feet to the water below.

*he dog, with its keen sense of smell,
was immediately aware of the presence of the
crocodile and sensed danger.*

Almost immediately the water exploded with a large splash and the dog let out a bloodcurdling cry.

It took the rancher only a moment to realize that the dog had been grabbed by a large crocodile that had been sunning itself below the bluff. The dog, with its keen sense of smell, was immediately aware of the presence of the crocodile and sensed danger. The dog had done the only thing he knew to do to keep his master from entering the water. He blocked his path and growled a warning. That failing, in total devotion to the person he loved, the dog sacrificed himself. What courage and devotion!

Do not despair. There is a happy ending to this story, at least for the dog and rancher. In barely a moment the rancher realized what was happening and quickly retrieved his revolver from its holster on the fencepost where he had hung it a few minutes earlier. He jumped into the water and dispatched the crocodile in time to save his best friend's life. The dog was torn a bit for the worse, but made a full recovery.

Stories of dogs and extraordinary events are more prevalent it seems than say cats, horses, and other common pets. This is understandable I suppose, because dogs are used in many service-oriented areas, such as K9 patrols, drug detection, ski patrols, and the like. Searching and finding seems to be a tailor-made role for canines, rather than for other animals. So stories of their accomplishments are much more numerous.

Take, for instance, the recent rescue of a lost toddler in the Northeast in subfreezing temperatures. It seems no one could find the lad, despite an intensive search. Rescuers began fearing that the cold would beat them to the child, so they called for more searchers. It did not help. Darkness fell and the search was called off until morning.

In desperation, the family dog was released into the night in hopes it might achieve what the rescuers could not. As the dog disappeared, no one actually believed it would do any good, but they were grasping at straws as the temperature dropped.

In the morning, searchers were up at first light. They found intermittent dog tracks and searched in the general direction the tracks seemed to lead. Expediency and determination seemed to have waned as all hope for finding the child alive disappeared with the setting sun the day before. Searchers moved almost lethargically through the brush and snow.

Several hours later, one of the rescuers let out a loud triumphant scream, "We found him, we found him alive." Excitement spread through the ranks of the searchers as rumors came down that the boy was still alive. And indeed he was. Half-exposed, half-pinned beneath the large family dog, the smiling face of the toddler peeked out at the first rescuer on the scene. The dog had not only located the boy, but had taken the matter under control by holding him down and providing warmth throughout the freezing night. The first searcher said it seemed the dog knew they would be coming and was holding the lad until they arrived.

Extraordinary stories may be dominated by dogs, but they are certainly not limited to that species. We have read stories of cats that warned their families of fire, carbon monoxide, and other dangers. How do they do these things? I can only suppose that they are driven by love and devotion. What other explanation will work?

I know that I made a distinction between wild animals and pets earlier, and my intention was to exclude the former to focus on the animals we interface with on a daily basis. However, sharing the above stories of courage and perseverance has brought to mind several other accounts of helpful animals that have impressed me throughout the years. Please indulge me while I briefly give credit to some of our non-pet friends of the animal kingdom. It will help solidify my contention that animals still retain a sense of companionship with us humans. I will explore this thought further in chapter 5.

Certainly you recall the very recent situation where a toddler fell into a gorilla enclosure and was knocked unconscious by the fall? To the amazement of all the horrified onlookers, the biggest beast in the pen moved over to the child, tenderly lifting him into her lap and cuddling him until help arrived. During the wait, she also fended off the attempts of some younger gorillas to play with the unconscious child. When the zookeepers arrived, she readily gave the child over to them. This was not an isolated incident. About a decade earlier, a similar situation had developed with basically the same result.

At least a few of you will recall the story of the woman from the Philippines who had found herself adrift in the Pacific Ocean after a boating mishap. Far from shore with no flotation device and virtually no hope of survival, she clung to life as long as she could. According to her personal account, when she was sure that she could tread water no longer, resigned that this was how her life was going to end, a large sea turtle surfaced within arm's reach. She grabbed hold of the turtle's shell and held on.

She managed to climb up partially on the back of the massive turtle. The animal did not seem to mind at all. Miraculously, the turtle stayed with her throughout the remainder of the day, through the evening and night hours and well into the next morning. She even managed to sleep for a few moments.

As light flooded the ocean the next morning, there was a ship on the horizon, a cruise ship it would later turn out, with hundreds of people (and therefore witnesses) on board. Unbelievably, the turtle began swimming in the direction of the ship. When turtle and ship met, the turtle began circling the ship, as if looking for a place to deposit his cargo. When a platform was lowered near the turtle, the turtle sounded (submerged), dislodging the woman, and it was not seen again. Many people witnessed this great event.

It is kind of spooky, isn't it? But when you consider the countless stories of porpoises saving swimmers and factor in the myriad accounts of animals providing services to people in so many ways, surely you can see that the original bond between man and animals still exists on some level, even in the wild.

This relationship between animals and people not only benefits us. There are many instances where people have gone to bat for animals, often at great risk to themselves. One particular story in the Topeka, Kansas, *Capital Journal* in January 1997 really moved me, causing me to think more seriously about this bond we have with animals. I was in town when it happened. I'll give you a brief version of the story that appeared in the newspaper on that day.

A local farmer had two horses. Actually, he probably had more, but the story was about these two particular horses, Shammy and Guyan. These two horses were siblings and lifelong companions to each other and the farmer for more than twenty-four years.

Shammy had fallen through the ice on the farmer's pond in sub-zero wind chill weather and was not able to climb out. He had fallen into a part of the pond that was over his head and it was all he could do to stand on his hind legs and get a breath. In fact, he was able only to poke part of his snout through the ice-clogged hole he had made in the ice with his fall. Even his eyes were underwater. The farmer had no idea that this had happened, but knew something was dreadfully wrong when Guyan came running up to the house, stomping and whinnying frantically. She was carrying on in a way that let him know something had happened to Shammy.

The farmer followed Guyan back down to the pond, assessed the situation, ran back to the house to call the fire department, and returned quickly to the pond to help hold Shammy's head above water. The fire department arrived and a successful rescue was mounted.

Later, when speaking with reporters, and much relieved that the incident had not resulted in tragedy, the farmer was quoted to have said, "I don't know what I would do if I had lost him, they are just like children to us." To quote another animal associated with Kansas, albeit fictional, "Ain't it the truth, ain't it the truth."

he picture of those two whales trapped and facing certain death as their air hole slowly froze over, and the hundreds of people rushing to their rescue, will stay with me forever.

And this case is not unique, but rather typical of the allegiance people feel toward animals. I am not talking about animal rights activists and the like, although they certainly care about animals. I am speaking rather of just everyday, common folk like you and me. How many times in the past few years have we picked up a newspaper or switched on the television to see hundreds of people giving their all to save groups of beached whales or porpoises? As I watched the people work feverishly to save them, my heart was in my throat and I wished I could have been a part of their effort. And what of the sea otters and turtles that the communities in California and the Florida Keys have spent tens of thousands of dollars on to repair missing flippers or broken bones? And what of the granddaddy of all acts of goodwill toward animals . . . the rescue of the two whales caught miles from the ocean in Alaska several years back?

How well I remember that episode. I followed it more closely than I did the Gulf War. The picture of those two whales trapped and facing certain death as their air holes slowly froze over, and the hundreds of people rushing to their rescue, will stay with me forever. The rescuers worked to cut holes in the ice for the whales to breathe, then moved a few dozen yards forward to cut other holes, while other people encouraged the whales to swim to them.

The progression moved forward hour after long hour, until

the entire landscape looked like the perforated line on a form. The whales eventually and gratefully swam out into open water, and I believe the entire nation rejoiced.

Though people and whales could not communicate, the people knew what was needed and the whales seemed to understand what was expected of them, as well. The many holes cut from love have long since frozen over again, but the picture of that day lives on in the memories of many and is a memorial to the goodwill of people toward animals and representative of the link we have with the animal world.

The people in these stories were driven by more than love of animals. Something deep inside tells us that we have a connection to the animals, not that we evolved from them, but that we were created with them. Certainly it is conceded that people benefit greatly from the companionship of animals. Studies have shown that people who share their lives with a pet generally live longer. There are programs today that place pets with residents of retirement homes because there is strong evidence that animals fill the emptiness and loneliness experienced by the elderly and lift their spirits. Quality and longevity of life is positively impacted when animals are part of the care.

But the door swings both ways in this relationship. Billions of dollars are spent on and for our pets each year. We pamper them and love them, clip them, comb them, and clean and powder them. We spend fortunes ensuring their good health. We have veterinarians, animal hospitals, specialists, and even animal psychologists. When we cannot afford or have not the place to keep an animal, some of us choose to adopt and sponsor them.

We sing songs about them, write books about them, compose

poetry and immortalize them in so many ways. There are no less than three major cable networks (such as Animal Planet) that run animal programs twenty-four hours a day (that is the literal Bible day, not the evolutionist's). There are dog shows and cat shows and horse shows and rabbit shows and pet expos and, well, I think you get the idea.

Surely we can see that God has an eternal plan for our animals.

We have a national network of helping hands like the Humane Society, SPCA (Society for the Prevention of Cruelty to Animals), and several other organizations who strive hard and do their best to rescue as many animals as possible. Then, there is the World Wide Web, where thousands of sites and hundreds of thousands of pages are dedicated to our wonderful animal friends. It is certainly a mutual relationship, one that both sides benefit from and enjoy.

In light of all this, and considering the evidence that follows, surely we can see that God has an eternal plan for our animals. I explore this subject much more deeply in the sequel to this book, so I won't go into detail here. Allow me to just say that God is not a God of the temporary. He does not make things on a temporary basis. I have already explained how this applies to the creatures He has made, but it applies also to the relationship He has forged between man and animal.

There is no doggy or kitty heaven. Similarly, there is no people heaven. There is God's heaven, that place where He dwells. He has made room for us and the angels. Surely you can see that He has made room for the other creatures He has made. Considering that He hung a billion planets on nothing, making room for all of us should prove to be no challenge for Him.

The question will undoubtedly be raised, "But where would He possibly fit all the animals that ever lived?" Well, for that matter, where would He fit all the people that ever lived? These are valid questions. Unfortunately, I cannot give you an exact answer because there is no scripture that speaks directly to this question. I am willing to speculate a little, though. Interestingly enough, during one of my many visits to the dentist years ago, I happened upon an article dealing with overpopulation. The article was written by someone with a whole lot more smarts than I on this topic. The author applied some mathematical equations to the known world population and came up with a unique and sobering conclusion. At least, it was sobering to me.

He concluded that the world wasn't as overpopulated as we might think. He justified that comment by saying that if it were possible to accomplish the task, there would be enough land surface in the state of Texas to accommodate a single family house for every living person (not family, mind you, but person) on earth. That is an amazing claim. Nevertheless, if you have been through that great state as many times as I have, you will have no trouble accepting his findings. It might be a bit crowded, but it sure looks like it could be done.

Now then, mentally form a picture of Texas in your mind. It is a large chunk of real estate, is it not? Now, surround Texas with the rest of the United States' mainland in that picture, and

all of a sudden Texas isn't all that big. Now, add the remainder
of North America. Then add South and Central America. Now,
add the other continents of the world, including the eleven-time-
zoned Soviet Union and the immense continent of Africa. Texas
seems to be quite small now.

Finally, take the sum of all that, which is our entire planet,
mix it into our solar system, and then the entire universe that we
are aware of, which consists of billions of stars and planets, some
thousands of times larger than our own, and I think that it is
very easy to see that God has more than enough room just in
the physical realm we are aware of, to house all of His living
creatures.

Chapter 3

COMMUNICATING

TALKING

Although unique and perhaps even revolutionary, I believe that the evidence presented thus far is an accurate representation of available fact. I put much effort and all of my heart into this work, spending long hours researching, praying, and meditating. I read everything on this subject that was available, and believe me, it was not much. Most of it was dated and hard to relate to today, such as C. S. Lewis's dissertation about animals and their souls.

I even queried the Library of Congress for similar manuscript information, but the kind ladies who searched for me could not find any copyrighted work. Consequently, my major source of information was the Bible. That may cause some to scrutinize my work with a bit more skepticism, but I welcome that scrutiny. I wish more people would check out what some individuals say in public more closely, rather than accepting their statements at face value. Our world would be a better place if everyone knew

certain facts firsthand, rather than relying on the way someone
else wants them to know them. I am sure that in my case, you
will find that I have not embellished on any of the facts set forth
in scripture.

That said, let me state with equal emphasis that what follows
in this chapter is without doubt speculation on my part. I have
little basis for my conclusions other than that it makes sense to
me based upon my research. I have no definite scriptural basis
for what I address in this chapter, but there are some scriptural
"hints," for lack of a better description.

There certainly is nothing that is in contrast with, or refutes,
my speculation, but that is not enough to prove that I am right.
I will leave it up to you to decide whether my ideas have merit.
At the very least, I hope I make you think about the possibilities I present.

Previously I told you that we will see our pets again. That is
factual, as far as I am concerned. My work has been challenged
by several fellow ministers, including the chancellor of a major
Christian university. They had never studied this out for themselves, but somehow still considered my ideas preposterous.
When I laid out the facts offered by scripture, many changed
their way of thinking. But some did not; however, they could no
longer argue with it, either. Honest people cannot change scripture. Rather, they are changed by it.

What would you think if I told you that I know we will see
our pets again, and it is possible that we may be able to converse
with them, as well? I can hear some of you now as you think
And how hard did you hit your head?

Admittedly, it is a bit off the beaten path of conventional

thought, perhaps even a bit bizarre. But please allow me the opportunity to explore the possibility with you, and allow yourself the chance to hear a new point of view. If you close your mind to a thought, please do so only after hearing it out and weighing any existing evidence. Often, the best lessons come from unconventional thoughts and actions. Long before the airplane ever flew, the concept of human flight was mocked and those who thought such thoughts considered possessed. Yet today, flight is routine, as evidenced by millions of people.

We lock ourselves in with tradition and routine. I am not condemning, either. I am merely suggesting that without creative thinking, new doors never open. Sometimes we open new doors and must shut them up again, and that is okay. But I think most of us want the chance of knowing what is on the other side before we permanently close that door. So, please accept this idea as it is intended—a speculation, a possibility. If you are still with me, you might as well continue on. It isn't going to hurt you and you might just enjoy what I have to say.

While I am quick to point out that this is speculation, it does not necessarily mean that I do not believe it to be a very real possibility. In fact, I do believe that animals can communicate. There are some very interesting things to consider. And that may be all they turn out to be . . . interesting. If that is the case, what have we lost by considering them? We have lost nothing but a few moments of our time.

But what if I am right? What if animals can talk? What an amazing eventuality that would be! Can you imagine the conversation you might carry on with the cat that you haven't seen in thirty years?

Now, before you echo the initial reaction of some of my colleagues and dismiss this idea as preposterous, please remember that previous to this point I used persuasive, factual approaches for every point I made. I was careful not to hazard a guess, unless I told you first that I was doing so. I have not changed my approach. I will not abandon logic or reasoning. I have already advised you that this section contains much speculation on my part. However, I also maintain that it could be, and probably is, true.

Consider what I have to say and draw your own conclusions. I cannot make you agree with me. If I could, I wouldn't, for this is simply my opinion. But it is an opinion based on evidences that are hard to dismiss. These thought-provoking evidences follow in no particular order.

Thought 1 . . .

Let's start in the beginning. I mean the beginning of time. Let's go back to the Garden of Eden. The devil, the Bible tells us, assumed the form of a serpent and spoke to Eve, tempting her to do something she was not supposed to do.

Eve responded to the serpent. In fact, a short conversation took place. I am not going to recount the conversation, for that really is not important to this section. Everyone has heard the story anyway. Instead, I want to point out that the most amazing thing about their conversation was that they had one at all.

How would you react if you came across a snake in your garden and it spoke to you? I am sure it would shake you up a little. Snakes aren't supposed to talk! Anyone would react with great alarm if an animal of any kind began a conversation with them. There is no indication, however, that Eve was at all taken aback by the serpent having the ability to speak. She didn't hesitate or wince in any way. Instead, she responded to him as if it were a normal occurrence, or as if it had happened many times before.

Eve was not shocked. She did not react as if it was something that should shock her. She did not react like you and I would react. The logical conclusion is to think it was not an unexpected thing, but one that was normal in their innocent world. Without a doubt, I believe both Adam and Eve had talked to this serpent before. On that I am not speculating. I do wonder, though, if the rest of the animals in the garden did not have the same ability of speech.

Thought 2 . . .

Many birds have the ability to speak . . . parrots, parakeets, ravens, crows, myna birds, and others. Some might contend that their speech capability is limited, and perhaps that is true. But I have seen some birds with almost insatiable appetites for learning new words.

A good friend of mine was working in a place where he allowed his own parrots to roam freely during business hours. One particular parrot, an African Gray by the name of Lola, was a remarkable bird. She could almost carry on a conversation with a person, and she had this talent of being able to duplicate sounds. She could emit sounds like a truck's backing warning signal, the television alert test signal, and a host of other sounds.

Lola's particular forte was imitating the ring of the telephone.

There was a portable phone in the shop and when it rang it was always a major undertaking to find it because people were all in the habit of leaving it wherever they finished their last conversation.

Lots of telephone calls came in during the day, and invariably when it rang, everyone would freeze and look around trying to remember where the phone was left last. Chaos took over as everyone raced around looking for it under this or that.

Apparently Lola enjoyed hearing the telephone ring. It seemed to break up the humdrum of the day for her by causing an exciting flurry of activity. So she took it upon herself to master the ring. No one encouraged her to do it, she just decided to do it on her own.

My friend doesn't know how long it took Lola to duplicate the sound, but he remembers clearly the day she chose to unveil this new talent. He and his coworkers were sitting around one day, when the phone rang. As usual, they jumped up, gave that stunned-deer-in-the-headlight look, and scrambled around looking for the portable. Someone found it, clicked it on, and said, "Hello." Then he threw the phone down and said, "I hate it when people hang up." No sooner had he thrown the telephone down, than it started ringing again. He picked it up again and said, "Hello" and threw it down again, this time cursing.

A few minutes later, it rang again and he made my friend pick it up. Again, there was nothing but a dial tone. But this time my friend had noticed that the phone and its base were to his left, but the ring had come from his right. It didn't take them long to figure out that the noise came from Lola. They decided to put the telephone down again and this time they watched her. Sure enough, it was her—busted!

They thought being discovered would make her stop, but they

were in for a surprise. She performed this little "trick" several dozen more times over the next couple of weeks. Each time the telephone rang they would look at her, and she would look so innocent that they answered the phone. Many times there was no one there and that innocent look quickly turned into a devious "gotcha" look.

They put their heads together and decided that no one would answer the phone on the first ring anymore. Oh, this bird was dealing with a brain trust now. True to the plan, when the phone rang, they waited for the second ring before answering it. As a side note, now that they were involved in this game with Lola, the telephone was never misplaced again. They kept it right in plain sight as they were eager to show that bird who she was dealing with. So with each second ring, whoever answered the telephone would, saying "hello," cover the speaker apparatus, turn to Lola, and say, "Not today, stupid," just to rub it in.

Imagine their surprise when just a day or two later, the telephone rang, they waited, it rang a second time, they answered, and found they had been suckered again. She had learned and adapted. She had apparently understood and accepted their challenge. She learned to ring twice, and even three times, with perfect intervals in between the rings.

But here is the kicker and the part that lends to my communication theory . . . this time, when she grinned at them with that devious "gotcha" grin, she added the words "Hello, stupid." Now, you may say she was just mimicking the words they said to her, but she wasn't. She took one of the words and added it to another to consciously and purposely mock them. (At least, that is the way it looked to me—I was there.)

Fortunately for the people in the store, she tired of the telephone game and moved on to other tricks, like disappearing out into the parking lot. She would wait for someone to come in the shop, slip through the door while the hydraulic closer eased the door shut. She did not fly; she walked everywhere. And she was not trying to escape. She had the life of a queen. She just liked walking out the door and coming back in later.

Apparently bored with just walking outside, she would go out and stand on top of someone's tire on their vehicle (under the fender well) and yell out loudly, "Where's Lola?" until someone found her. What a personality.

Then, returning to evidence of animal communication, there was the time I was showering in my home in Hawaii many years ago. I was just scrubbing away and almost at that point where one breaks out in song, when from out of nowhere came this unfamiliar voice saying, "Good morning." Completely surprised, I tried covering myself with my hands thinking someone was in the bathroom with me . . . and someone I did not know at that.

I looked out of the shower stall and there was no one there. I couldn't imagine where the voice was coming from because I was alone in the bathroom and it was on the second floor. Then they said it again, "Good morning." I looked in the direction from where the voice had come and my eyes came to rest on the two-screened panel windows above the shower (temperatures in Hawaii rarely go low enough to require closing the windows, and installed screens allow steam to escape).

I squinted to look through the screen and there on the pinnacle of some sort of protrusion on the roof, was a myna bird, a bird with a painted grin on its face that makes it look like it is always smiling. If you have ever been to Hawaii, you could not possibly forget that grin or the goofy hop hop hop step they make (a lot like the Heckle and Jeckel magpie cartoon characters).

I looked at him and he said it again, "Good morning," and gave me one of those head-twisting looks. I returned his "Good morning" and he hopped closer to the screen window. He actually looked like he was going to start a conversation. Instead, he simply repeated his salutation, twisted his head a few more times, and then flew off, presumably to peep at someone else in the shower.

It was an interesting encounter. For a few moments I wondered to myself if the bird actually knew what he was saying, but I really didn't care about such things in those days, so my mind quickly wondered in another direction. Today, reflecting back, I wonder about birds and this ability they have to speak. Is it just an ability to mimic the sounds they hear, or is it a leftover attribute from an earlier ability to communicate intelligently?

Thought 3 . . .

Animals communicate with each other. This is a fact we must acknowledge. We see it happen before our eyes almost on a daily basis . . . dogs barking, birds chirping, cats meowing, and so on. Science has documented many forms of communication between animals. Some of the methods they employ are more complicated than others, but all are effective means of communication.

Commonly, this communication comes in the form of an audible sound, but sometimes it is silent (at least to the human ear). Some creatures use a whistling sound or a series of clicks, grunts, or growls. Others, like dolphins and bats, send out high-frequency

It is not outrageous, then, for me to say that animals "talk."

sound waves that are interpreted by others with the appropriate receiving apparatus.

Whatever means are used, there is no denying that animals communicate with each other, and that they do so effectively. Other animals know exactly what is being said to them. It is not outrageous, then, to say that animals "talk." Talking is simply a form of communication, the relaying of your thoughts to another. The thoughts do not have to assume the form of words that you and I understand to qualify as "talking," they merely have to be understood by the receiver.

Truth be known, animals are sometimes more effective communicators than human beings. Now, I did not say, nor do I mean, that they are more intelligent or have a vocabulary equal to ours. I merely said they are more effective at times. That is because, unlike humans, animals always communicate what they mean. There is no pretense with their "speech" as there is with human communication.

Often, we humans will say something that could have more than one meaning. For instance, a curious fellow employee might ask innocently, "Gee, I wonder how Molly got that job?" She was just expressing curiosity. Another employee, motivated by jealousy, might respond more suggestively, "Yeah, I wonder what she did to get that job!" We witness innuendos like this all the time. In fact, we are probably guilty of them ourselves.

Not so animals. They are straight-shooters. How many of you have ever been deceived by your cat? She purred after you stroked her, but you know she didn't really enjoy it. She was putting you on to stay on your good side. Of course she enjoyed it . . . cats cannot help but purr in pleasure or wag their tails when irritated. It is their nature.

How many of you have come home to a lying dog? Well, I suppose I ought to rephrase that question. I am sure many of us come home to find the dog lying on the floor, or on the couch, or in the easy chair. What I mean is how many of you have ever come home to find a dog that tried to lie to you? I mean he was in a real bad mood. His day was awful. He had several accidents on the carpet, went for his annual rabies shot, and even had to endure yet another bowl of dry dog food!

He didn't feel like running to the door to greet you. He didn't want to have to put on that dumb happy face act again like he has so many other times. His tail was sore from the shot and he just couldn't possibly wag it right now. But he knew that was what you were expecting, so he came running to the door, jumping and wagging that tail for you. He even beat it against the wall a few times, "thump, thump, thump" because he knows that makes you laugh. And then when you bent down to pat him on the head, he slobbered all over you, wagging that sore tail "ouch, ouch, ouch." What a big fibber!

When animals communicate, they mean what they say. We could learn a lesson from them.

Obviously these are not serious questions or situations. Animals simply do not lie. Now sometimes they might bluff, as in the case of a mother protecting her young and growling. She may even fake a charge at a perceived threat to her offspring when someone gets too close. But actually, they aren't really bluffing, but rather giving a warning. And that warning is real. There is no pretense to it. Take the warning or suffer the consequence is the message being sent. When animals communicate, they mean what they say. We could learn a lesson from them. What a better world this would be if everyone learned to speak honestly.

A simple termite colony runs better than the largest city ever built, minus the crime and poverty.

Even insects communicate. Some of their societal networking is so intricate and so much more efficient than our own that one wonders how anyone could believe that we humans are so much more "evolved." A simple termite colony runs better than the largest city ever built, minus the crime and poverty.

Animals do communicate. They speak in many ways, by color and appearance, by posture or gesture, and audibly and inaudibly. They speak to each other and they speak across species lines. They also speak to humans. We may not always understand them, but often we do.

My little Westie had a difficult time learning that she wasn't supposed to piddle in the house. Eventually the light went on and she said, "Oh, that is what you have been trying to tell me."

She then learned how to tell me it was time to perform that function so that I would open the door and let her outside. The longer she waited to tell me, the more excited her communication would become. If I listened to what she was saying, everything went well. But when I didn't listen, well, it was time for the paper towels. And this story leads me to my next thought.

Thought 4 . . .

Pets communicate with their people. In fact, most, if not all, animals that are associated with people communicate, or try to communicate, with people. For example: dolphins and whales have a discernible language. They use their language very effectively. Large groups of them travel and live together in great harmony because they can speak to one another. Hunter groups work together to herd schools of fish, matriarchs protect offspring by telling them where to swim in the pod, and we could enumerate many other examples if needed. We have managed to decode and document their language. We have even managed to duplicate the sounds they use in order to speak back to these creatures in a language they understand.

As I pen these words, my terrier is doing a little dance in front of me with her pull toy dangling from her mouth.

Admittedly, their language isn't very complicated, but it is effective and it works for them. It works for us, as well. We replicate the sound-words and they respond to their trainers in the desired way. We have also elevated their communicative abilities by teaching them part of our language via sight and sound signals.

Our household pets have proven to be equal, if not superior, to our ocean mammal friends. They learn quickly to communicate their thoughts to us. As I pen these words, my terrier is doing a little dance in front of me with her pull toy dangling from her mouth. I have no doubt what she is trying to communicate to me. She has several dances that she performs, each with a different meaning. There is no mistaking the meaning of the dance she is doing at the moment, because of the toy or other item she has in her mouth. When she wants me to understand what she wants to do, she delivers her message very effectively.

I now am faced with three possible choices, one of which I must communicate back to her. I can stop what I am doing and reach for her toy, which will make her very happy, but take me from my work. I can tell her, "No, not now," and her ears will drop along with her toy and she will walk off with a very sad countenance. In fact, she will overemphasize the sadness. They can be such actors. Finally, the choice I opt for . . . I can simply continue typing, which she will eventually interpret as, "Not now, maybe later." She will then either curl up at my feet and wait or she will start playing by herself. Whatever option I take, we have both effectively communicated to each other.

We all know that this type of interchange is not limited to dogs. Many, if not all, animals have this capacity, especially those that are domesticated. I once had a kitten that made the same demands upon me as the dog I mentioned above. Her toy was a string with a small piece of cloth wadded up and tied to one end.

She loved to paw this wad of cloth. I kept her toy on top of my dresser in the bedroom. If I went in the bedroom for any reason, she would jump up on my dresser, snatch her toy, jump down on the bed, and bother me until I gave in and played. She did not meow once, but she communicated her thoughts to me quite adequately.

No doubt you remember television commercials where they show a dog or cat apparently talking. Some are obviously staged and the videos doctored. Others are merely common pets that make uncommon or unusual sounds. One local roofing company asked the dog in their advertisement, "What are we best at fixing," and the dog of course responded, "Roof," or something close enough to it to make you think it did.

The idea was simple and effective. People love animals and they enjoy humor . . . so when you combine the two, it is bound to be a hit. Another video used on one of those home video programs spoofed a cat that was being given a bath in a tub. The cry of the cat was captured on the video as it struggled to get away from the person washing it and out of the tub. The cry was an unmistakably drawn out "Noooooooooooooooo." I realize that the cat was not actually saying the word. Rather it was uttering an irritated version of its "meow." Or was it?

Am I suggesting that animals can say words? Of course certain animals can say words. Take the myna bird I spoke of before. The real question is, "Do they consciously pick the words they say because they know what they mean?" I honestly do not know. One could make a convincing argument either way. Let me share one made by a very dear friend of mine.

He had a very intelligent cairn terrier who he swears used

words all the time. For instance, when the dog wanted to go outside to take care of business, it would sit in front of one of the family members and say, "Out." They swear that the dog used the word in the same way they used it when training her as a puppy. The word uttered by the dog was a bit more drawn out, so that it sounded more like "ooooouuuuuuu." Obviously the dog had trouble forming the "t," but my friend swore the tone and emphasis resembled the word they had always used.

Of course, to be cordial, I gave him a cursory, "Uh huh," and let it go at that. A talking dog indeed! I was not convinced. Imagine my surprise when visiting in my friend's home many years later, the dog sat in front of us and said, "oooouuuu." There was no doubt in my mind that the dog was speaking to us. It was quite amazing. I half expected the dog to say, "Thank you" when it came back into the house.

I have encountered many people with dogs, cats, and other pets, who assure me that their pets genuinely try to communicate with them.

Since that time, I have encountered many people with dogs, cats, and other pets, who assure me that their pets genuinely try to communicate with them. I mean the animals actually are trying to form words. I have had many, many pets, but have never been as fortunate as some of these folks. All my pets prefer their own "tongue" to that of humans. None have been bilingual. Nevertheless, their ability to communicate their thoughts and emotions to me has not been diminished. By using sounds, body language, and gestures, they have adequately communicated to me.

Thought 5 . . .

There are numerous references to animals in heaven in the Bible. That is well known by anyone who regularly spends time in this book. Little attention is paid to the "other" creatures mentioned in the book of the Revelation and some Old Testament books.

These creatures appear to be a form of animal as much as anything else. In fact, my speculation is that they are a cross between animal and angelic being, but I can offer no proof for that opinion, only my own impression. I explore this opinion and offer more evidences in the sequel to this book, which is in the works; therefore, we will not discuss it here at length.

Now, the word *animal* does not appear anywhere in scripture. Instead, the word(s) *beast, creature, creeping things, everything that has breath*, and so forth, are used. Therefore, speculating that these "other creatures" are related to animals, in part or whole, is not a great stretch. Certainly they are not human.

What type of animal they are is not important. What is important to our study is that they speak. They use audible, understood words in worship of God the Father. More important, it appears this is not an uncommon or unique occurrence in scripture. A serpent spoke to Adam and Eve, a donkey spoke to a prophet, and these creatures in the Apostle John's presence.

Thought 6 . . .

Revelation, chapter 5, verse 13, says:

> *And every creature which is in heaven, and on the*
> *earth, and under the earth, and such as are in the*
> *sea, and all that are in them,* heard I saying,
> *Blessing, and honor and glory, and power, be unto*
> *him that sitteth upon the throne and unto the*
> *Lamb forever and ever.*

There is so very much to discuss about this verse, most of which I will withhold for later chapters. It is important to note here, however, that portion of the verse that I placed in italics. The Apostle John, who authored this book under the direction of God, said, "heard I saying." In other words, he heard the creatures (animals) speak. I realize that this word is inclusive of humans as well, but if you will study all the elements of this verse, you can only conclude that it is speaking of ALL creatures created by God.

Now, remember that this is a prophetic book about future things and this has not yet come to pass, but will one day. Nevertheless, it is a very solid piece of evidence that animals have the ability to speak. The evidence "speaks" for itself.

Conclusion

Are any of these thoughts overwhelmingly convincing as to the ability of animals to speak? No. Independently, each thought comprises some fact and some speculation. Taken by itself, with the exception of thought number six, each thought is a weak argument.

Collectively, however, they give us considerable cause to believe that animals have the ability to speak, or at least once did. These thoughts mesh together to give us a preponderance of the evidence, which is one of the criteria used in our legal system of proof. The evidence is not undeniable, but it is very convincing. Far less evidence has been accepted to establish religious dogma on more important issues.

Acceptance of this idea boils down to the open-mindedness of the individual weighing the evidence. Human nature is a peculiar thing in regards to what we believe. Once a person has adopted their set of beliefs on a particular issue, it is very difficult to convince them otherwise, regardless of mounting evidence for an opposing view. If, therefore, you are not yet convinced, I hope at least you have come to the point where this idea is less radical to you than it was when you began this chapter. I will leave off making a case on this issue for now, but will pick it up again in chapter 5.

BODY LANGUAGE

I find it very difficult to deal with the memories of departed pets, even though I am certain that I will one day see them again. I have never handled separations well. Bidding a temporary farewell to our pets is similar to leaving the people you love when you must travel. You know you will be reunited in a few days or weeks, but it is difficult to be separated from those you are accustomed to being with.

As a young man during the Vietnam era, I found myself stationed aboard the USS *Forrestal* (CVA 59), an attack aircraft carrier stationed in Norfolk, Virginia, at the time. As a new husband and young father, it was difficult to endure the long six- or seven-month deployments away from home. I made two and a half such cruises and several lesser-length deployments in between, which were required to keep the crew and equipment prepared and seaworthy. We all knew we had an important job to do for our country by keeping a vigil in strategic waters, but that did little to lessen the loneliness one feels when away from family and friends. Despite the fact that there were more than 5,000 other men on board, you couldn't help but feel alone sometimes.

It was always great to head home. I remember the ship showed movies on the closed-circuit network on board for seventy-two solid hours while making the three-day transit from the Azores to Norfolk. Those in charge knew most everyone could not sleep, so they provided entertainment to keep us occupied. We were zombies when we arrived home, but such was the life of a sailor. Those of you who have been deployed while serving in a nautical service know what a thrill it is to dock at homeport and see thousands of loved ones cheering your ship in.

Remembering and missing loved ones who have passed is much like being away on a trip. You know you will see them again, and you count the days until that great reunion. The same is true of the pets we have lost. They are family to us and we miss them dearly. The difference is that the separation is usually a lot longer than that of a deployment and you must deal with the memories and the waiting for a lifetime. And memories can be very difficult to handle at times.

This section is about our pets' abilities to communicate with us through the use of body language. Sensitivity toward your pet is an absolute must if you are going to interpret what they are saying. I have observed insensitive people missing the boat with pets they claim they love.

Many people neglect their pets in this area of communication. They may feed and water them, walk them, take them regularly to the clinic, and do all the things necessary to provide for and protect them. But if they are not communicating with their pets, they are neglecting a very important need. Pets need to talk to us. They have emotions and ideas they want to communicate to us. Imagine how frustrating it is when they are eager to say something, but no one is paying attention!

One cannot be sensitive in one thing and not in another. Sensitivity, therefore, is a requirement for someone who truly wants to communicate with their pet. I do not mean by this that you have to be a boo hoo baby like me when it comes to romantic things, although there is nothing wrong with that. I simply mean that you must be sensitive enough to the needs of others, human and animal, to be able to recognize certain body language. I know when my wife is sad without her ever telling me. I certainly know when she is upset with me before she ever has to spell it out. Body language and gestures are important to a good relationship, and sensitivity is the instrument that allows you to perceive and interpret the signals. If you do not enjoy a communicative relationship with your pet, you must work on your sensitivity and awareness.

Animals need us to be sensitive to their attempts to communicate. We are as important to them as they are to us. When your
best friend is pawing at your leg while you are watching the news,
he is trying to tell you something. When they do their little "dance"
or if they just sit in front of you and stare, there is probably a
message to be received. When an animal tries to communicate,
the body language can take any number of forms. But when they
are successful, and see that you got the message and are going
to react appropriately, the body language is usually predictable.
They jump for joy and act silly. It is my opinion that it isn't so
much they realize they are getting what they were asking you for
(i.e., water, food, a walk), but more that they are gleeful for having talked to you.

One of our current babies, who I mentioned earlier as my
West Highland white terrier named "Missy," is quite the cutie,
possessing an extremely sweet nature. She brightens up our home.
And is she ever smart! (I hope there is some truth to the notion
that pets reflect the attributes of their people.)

She is just a sweetheart . . . just about the perfect dog, quickly
fitting into the family unit and adding so much joy and happiness to our lives. Don't laugh at me, but I sometimes take my
lunch hour and rush back home the twelve miles just to throw
the ball for her a couple of times. Physically, she is your typical
Westie, with a pretty white coat and stout and alert countenance.
She has one deformity however . . . a very pronounced overbite.
We saw an advertisement in the paper—the breeder was going
to probably put her down if someone did not rescue her, because
she did not measure up to their standards. I do not mean to sug-

gest that all breeders are of this caliber, for there are some very good ones . . . but there are some very bad ones, too.

Back to point, her overbite has caused her no discomfort and is not a problem for us. However, she (and we) discovered that her overbite causes a very peculiar snapping or popping sound when she bites at something and misses. As a puppy she would bite at a hand or toy in play and in missing, her jaws would clamp shut on nothing but air. This would create a unique popping sound and a very humorous situation for the family.

When Missy discovered that her popping sound made us laugh and that after we laughed at her we would hug her, she quickly capitalized on this good fortune. When she wanted something or when she got herself in trouble, she would employ her popping sound, prancing around, turning her head from side to side, and snapping her jaws shut, "pop, pop, pop."

In no time she developed the noise into a sort of language, which she accentuated with body movements and gestures. She has now mastered several "acts," each employing all of the above-mentioned antics, but each also distinctly different, performed for different reasons. One act means she wants food or water. Another means she wants to go outside. Another means it is play time.

I know you will raise an eyebrow, but once in a while she doesn't want anything from me but to just talk. I will be sitting at the computer, perhaps answering questions readers send to me, and in the silence of the room, she "pops off," so to speak.

She has food and water, and we already played. She has her own door to go outside when she wants. There is no need being expressed, except that she wants to talk. So I will talk a little human to her, and then I will mimic her popping sound, which seems to excite her even more (I wonder what it is I said).

Each of the pets this family has shared their lives with has had quite unique personalities, which in turn gave them uniquely different ideas on how to communicate. Without exception, all have employed body language—sounds and gestures to communicate with us—and we have been sensitive enough to have known they were doing so. Only those who have kept and loved a pet of their own and who have been sensitive to them can truly appreciate that animals have more than an ability to communicate . . . they have a need. When you couple this interpersonal behavior with their wonderful personalities and devotion, it makes their companionship more desirable than some humans we have known.

It is usually for these reasons that people prefer to keep pets. They are exposed to the cute antics and body language . . . the almost bewitching looks animals are so famous for giving. They communicate love and devotion without ever saying the words. Before you know it, that pet has a permanent place in your heart and home.

Once in the home, the animal almost invariably bonds quickly and more closely than one could imagine. Homes are enriched by this addition and family bonds made stronger. In time, this nonhuman personality becomes part of the human family and learns how to communicate with other family members. It makes for a wonderful relationship and is the reason why many first-time pet people become lifelong pet people. If your animal does not appear to be communicating with you, I suspect they are, but you are not listening.

LISTENING

The process involved with mailing a very important letter is probably a good representation of how the mechanics of communication work. Communication, in any form, cannot be considered successful unless the intended audience receives the intended message. If that important letter does not get placed in the right mailbox and delivered to the right person, the effort to communicate fails. In oral communication, the same principle applies. The message can be transmitted, but if it is not heard, it really cannot be considered successful communication.

If the pet/human relationship is to be successful, it is important that we listen to our pets. Likewise, it is fundamental that pets listen to us and understand what we are saying. Since pets depend upon us for sustenance and protection more than we rely on them for what they contribute to the relationship, it is paramount that we exercise a modicum of control over their daily activities. We do that by communicating effectively to them.

While some may balk over my use of the term *control*, it is precisely that control that keeps them out of danger as they live in our world. Let me give you an example of what I mean.

I was jogging one sunny afternoon in Miami, far outside the city in an area known as horse country. As I worked my way along a very scenic road, I noticed two large dogs running toward me from deep inside a very large and unfenced yard on the opposite side of the street. They were coming toward me from about 200 feet away at a very quick pace.

Although they were barking and charging, they did not appear to be ferocious. It seemed they were more bent on making a point than attacking me. They wanted me to know that they were defending their master's property from all intruders, including the dreaded jogger.

I have absolutely no fear of dogs anyway. I was more concerned about their safety than I was my own. If I was on the other side of the road nearest them, it would not be a problem, but calculating their speed and determination, I knew they would not stop at the natural border of their yard. They were certainly planning to cross the street to make sure I knew they were on the job.

However, they did not know there was a car coming down the road at a fairly good clip that looked as if it was going to arrive at their point of crossing just about the same time as they would. There was nothing I could do to get the attention of the oncoming car's driver in time, so I did the only thing I could do. I stopped, faced the dogs, and yelled loudly in a very demanding and authoritative voice, "**STOP!**"

Both dogs stopped in their tracks, almost in cartoon fashion, with their legs slipping underneath them. They stopped just before reaching the asphalt road, at almost precisely the same moment the car went whizzing by. The dogs looked at each other as if to say, "Man, he's mean . . . and he is on the other side of the street after all." They then turned back toward the house and disappeared from sight, never knowing how close to tragedy they had come. I was very happy to have been of service to those animals. I am happy also that their owner had taken the time to communicate with them and teach them obedience to commands.

Animals we allow to live in our world with us are subject to dangers they usually are not aware of, and listening to us is so very important. The outcome of the situation I just relayed was favorable due in large part to the dogs' ability to listen and understand, which I am sure is a result of their people taking time to condition them to do so. I think about those beautiful dogs now and then and wonder if their luck is still holding. I certainly hope so.

Their story helps me illustrate my point. Animals are able to listen and understand. I am not saying that they sit around all day thinking, I hope my master tells me to roll over later, but once the request to do so is made, they remember and are able to discern what is meant. Habit or conditioning? Perhaps. However, I think it is more.

It is exactly this ability to understand and respond in the animals we adopt as our pets that cause us to accept and love them. There are exceptions, though—some pets do not possess that capacity, not even if we incredibly stretch the criteria.

Reptiles, amphibians, and fish, for instance, do not communicate with humans in the true sense of the word as we have used it in this study. Through repetition, they may know when it is time to eat and they become more active and responsive at those times. They may even recognize or actually tolerate the presence of one human over another. Their apparent excitement and their ability to distinguish the difference in people is due to the sustenance they anticipate rather than preference of one person to another.

Do they love us? As an amateur herpetologist, with much experience in the field of reptiles and amphibians, I am compelled to say that they do not. We certainly get attached to them. We certainly grieve their passing. But we do not hold them in as high regard as a pet that can reciprocate our affections with love for us. Even the reptile that enjoys the best reputation for co-habitation with humans, the iguana, falls far short of the capacity of some of the lowliest mammals.

Take, for instance, the domestic rat. To most people, the little gray, tan, and white mammals are not much different from their wild cousins who scour the sewers and garbage heaps for a living. They see them as nasty, disgusting creatures. Not so! Oh, I admit they are not very clean animals and often they can be mean, inflicting nasty bites. I have been on the receiving end of their incisors on many occasions. They are defensive and if not accustomed to close human contact, they can and will bite.

More frequently, however, domestic rats are much more friendly than most people think. Social creatures by nature, they fit very well into our world as pets, very much like a cat or dog. The inherent problems are that they do not readily housebreak, they have poor hygiene, and their life expectancy is short. Still, many people swear by them as good pets. They can show affection and respond to commands. They are loyal creatures that have been known to defend their people from perceived threats. I knew one little girl who had a wonderful relationship with her pet rat. In fact, it slept at the foot of her bed each night. While the little girl slept, the otherwise peaceable creature would not even let Mom and Dad near the bed to tuck the girl in.

The point is, those pets we surround ourselves with (and admittedly, I speak of mammals and birds almost exclusively in this section) listen to us, sometimes intently. They learn to respond to commands and requests by repetition, but they also can understand and respond to what is being said the very first time.

It depends on the individual. I suspect animals are like people in that regard. Some folks are less intelligent than others. Some folks focus on different interests, so that we are motivated by some things, but slow to show interest in others. The average household pet that has not benefited from some sort of obedience training is no different.

Animals are also often innovative. We may ask them to fetch a ball and they wind up bringing us several. Or they may bring us something else that it is of more interest to them. Or they may not do anything at all, simply because they do not feel like it.

My dogs know what "get the ball" means. It means we are going to play. And that is a lot of work for me because two of three of my dogs like to play ball and they are very competitive. I have to throw a ball alternately for each of them to chase down, while ensuring they remain separated.

Usually they are eager to play, but once in a great while they aren't. They just want to sleep or they are busy doing something else. I know they hear me and understand, but they just aren't interested. They have an amazing capacity for fathoming what we are saying.

Now, this does not mean that we can say to them "please go

get my oxfords, third drawer of my dresser in the blue room down the hall" and expect them to be successful. There is a limit to their capacity. However, when we say "go" or "come" most pets, be they dogs, cats, horses, or birds, already know what is expected. It is part conditioning by repetition, but it is also part recognition of the word and understanding its meaning.

How well they interpret what follows action words depends upon how perceptive we are as to their capacity to understand and/or their desire to respond. A new puppy or kitten will not have the familiarity with words that an older animal has, but they have an eager spirit. A dog that seldom exercises, or an older cat, probably will be lethargic and pretty much unresponsive to most action words. They will listen and understand, but it might take a stick of dynamite to make them move. But a dog that is often tasked to learn and play will be eager to listen and respond.

Take my Westie for example. When I find the time to play, she is always eager and ready. She responds quickly, sometimes too quickly. I want to tell her "go get the ball," but upon hearing the word "go," she is gone, responding to the action word without waiting for the identifier. Consequently, she races through the house and comes back with the first of her toys that she encounters.

I show slight disapproval and say, "No, I said go get the . . . ," but again, before I say the word *ball*, she hears the "go," drops whatever she is holding, and again races off into toyland looking for something else.

If it happens to be the ball that she finds on this latest journey, all is well and the communicating ends and we play. If not the ball, I repeat the "no" again and give her a stern look. It appears to me that the gesture has the intended effect on her as she sits quietly trembling with anticipation, waiting for my next words. At least, that is how it appears to me. It may very well be that she is thinking What an idiot—why can't he make up his mind already?

Whatever the case may be, I take a bit of a different approach the third time. I look at her and give her the identifier first, "ball—go get the ball." In this way I know she got the spherical picture of the ball before she got the action word. As with the other times, she takes off in a flash, but this time comes back with a ball. I have spoken and she has listened, received the message and acted appropriately upon it.

We have seen this "listening" work with dogs, cats, cows, monkeys, horses, pot belly pigs, and a variety of other mammals. It is communicating in the very simplest form, but it is communicating nonetheless.

I would hazard to say it is on the same level as a person from Germany speaking to a person from China, neither of them understanding the other's language. They need to communicate, but each only knows a few keywords and phrases from the other's language. They are forced to rely upon gestures, tone, and body language to augment the few words they know. It is usually a very funny scene to see people with different tongues trying to communicate. Often they think speaking slowly or more loudly will help. In the end, pointing and gesturing and using known words is what brings about successful communicating.

Though not the best example, I think it is similar to how our pets learn to communicate with us (and we with them). We do not speak each other's language, so we learn keywords (or in their

Animals may no longer possess the ability to speak, if in fact they ever had it at all, but they do still listen and understand.

case sounds), learn to interpret body language and tone, and somehow arrive at that point where we understand each other.

Animals may no longer possess the ability to speak, if in fact they ever had it at all, but they do still listen and understand. Their level of understanding may vary from animal to animal, but when an animal bonds with people, they most certainly are attentive when those people communicate with them. Some focus so passionately on listening that we feel inclined to hold complete conversations with them.

Cats are prone to sit and listen to their humans for long periods of time, and they often show great interest in what is being said. Readers report to me that their cat will purr when they are telling them about a pleasant experience or swish their tail the way cats do when they speak of something that bothers them. Some may attribute this to a reaction by the animal to voice inflections, but that is too convenient an explanation. There is much more substance to their reaction than a perception of mood. If it were just that, it would be evident only at the moment of exchange, but often the family pet's mood will mirror the prevailing mood in the family unit. Your world overlaps theirs. What upsets you upsets them.

I had one wonderful old cat who would listen so intently that I thought he was going to answer me. When I sounded glad, he seemed glad and vice versa. I know he somehow perceived my mood and reacted to it, but as anyone who has kept cats knows, they also understand your words. They are intelligent and perceptive creatures.

Perhaps a less impeachable example is needed. As I told you earlier, not long ago we lost one of the finest pets we have ever had, and we lost her prematurely. She was a beautiful Chihuahua, just an adorable and trusting dog. She had all the typical Chihuahua traits of being afraid of thunder (and visibly shaking when it occurred), cowering in fear when the windshield wipers came on in the car, hiding when someone new dropped by, and spending much time under a blanket to stay warm.

A few days after this tragic loss occurred, I was sitting in my bedroom weeping in grief. Apparently my weeping was a bit loud as my young Westie overheard me and came running into the room turning her head from side to side in that way that dogs do when they hear something that perplexes them.

Let me pause momentarily to emphasize again that this happened when my Westie was young. This puppy had never been able to refrain from the things puppies do. She bit everything that came within reach . . . toes, fingers, electric cords, doors, and walls. Her name is Missy, as I mentioned earlier, but because of her propensity for chewing things, we dubbed her "Missy the Monster." I am not exaggerating when I say she could *never* stop biting.

Moreover, she could never sit still. It was zoom over to the window, chew on the curtain cord, zoom back to the couch, chew on the foot connected to that man, zoom over to the edge of the carpet and chew on that. She had an endless supply of energy and a mission to chew the world into oblivion. I honestly can-

Missy

not remember ever seeing her asleep or without something in her mouth that was not supposed to be there.

On this occasion, however, she came into the room, took one look at me, heard this strange sound coming from her "play-friend," jumped on the bed, and snuggled right up to me and licked my hands. She then looked up into my eyes and I swear, by her expression and focus, if she could have spoken, she would have said "I know you miss Pebbles. I do too. But we still have each other. Can't you be happy again? Don't cry. I love you."

She put her head in my lap and just laid there, no biting, no jumping around, nothing! She just lay still as I wept, occasionally tenderly licking my hands as I stroked her, until I finally emptied myself of tears and composed myself. She remained like this throughout the twenty minutes of my blues and never tried to leave. She also did not attempt to chew, bite, or play.

The behavior was so out of character for her or for any puppy for that matter. When I spoke about the loss of our mutual friend, she listened. I mean she really listened. Oh not *as if* she understood . . . she *definitely* understood. Her eyes seemed to say "I know, I know." And her sober mood and placid behavior told me that she was grieving with me.

So there is no misunderstanding or doubt about the significance and uniqueness of her behavior, immediately after this encounter, she went back to being Missy the Monster and resumed her quest to chew the world apart. But for the time I needed her to listen, she did so.

They hear and listen, my friend, and they understand.

Chapter 4

LIFE

Perhaps the most difficult task I faced in producing this book was deciding upon the correct placement of this chapter. By the time you read this, it probably will have had several different numerical designations. I even thought to exclude it, because I know it will not be well received by everyone. But since the subject of this chapter is more crucial to my case than any other information I have given you, it was imperative that it be included.

Nevertheless, it remains a very difficult subject to address. There is more potential for skepticism here than in any other part of the book. I fully expect to suffer some ridicule over what I say, but do not welcome it. Despite that threat, I feel very strongly about the thoughts I will pass on to you here. I am certain that if I can articulate them correctly, you will be compelled to agree with most of what I have to say. This puts a big monkey on my back, for I know that you truly cannot please everyone, even when you desire to do so.

There are many aspects we could discuss on the subject of

life. Probably, most everyone would prefer to be told what the meaning of life is. Perhaps my comments in chapter 6 will help you in that regard. Others might wonder about life on other planets. Still others might be concerned about the quality of life on our own planet and related environmental issues.

Unfortunately, as important as those issues might be, they really do not fit into our theme. So we will pass on them and forge ahead to address a much larger issue. Specifically, I want to ask, and answer a question that is seldom addressed, namely, "What is life?"

That may seem like a very elementary question, but it is one that may cause you to do a little more thinking than you may have expected to do as we progress through the answer. As you explore this issue with me, it will hopefully occur to you that this is a subject we take for granted, but one that we should thoroughly understand because it carries with it such important spiritual implications.

Let us begin our quest for this answer in a place where most of us acknowledge that human and animal life began, the Garden of Eden. Even many non-Christian cultures allude to life beginning in such a garden, so this should not be hard for most readers to agree with. It was here, according to the Bible and Christian and Jewish faiths, that God originally housed the work of His hands. We will not discuss the actual act of creation in detail as that information is more than adequately covered in a much greater book than this. Rather, let us explore the facts we know about God's plan for the living creatures He created.

God's original plan for this world was that it should be perfect . . . that mankind should be perfect and that we should live forever. The perfect plan also included animals, and in keeping with the longevity considerations of that plan, they too were made perfect and intended to live without ever dying. Neither people nor animals would age or suffer disease under God's plan.

Of course we know that all of that changed when man launched his own plan and disobeyed the Lord. The point we need to see is that animals were part of the big plan. In fact, they were necessary, perhaps crucial elements to it. They were so important to the habitat of mankind that God made them first so that they would be in place when people arrived.

Animals were created for many reasons. The most important reason for their creation was to provide companionship to Adam, and therefore mankind, throughout the ages. This companionship pleased Adam and made him happy.

Lest we forget this very important fact, animals were made for God's pleasure, too. God created them with His own hands and to do so brought Him great pleasure. We are told that after God surveyed everything He made, He assessed it as being "very good."

We are to interpret this to mean that the animals were exactly as God wanted them to be (as if there was any doubt). It may be difficult from this side of the fall of mankind to look at wasps, ants, snakes, and skunks to see what God saw when He called them very good, but originally they were.

Originally wasps did not sting and skunks did not fumigate. Back then, they were the companions of mankind. Adam and Eve embraced the creatures made by God's hand and the animals reciprocated with affection for them. Neither man nor animal ate meat. There was no killing and no death. They and the animals ate fruit and grain and vegetables.

I am not sure what they did for entertainment in the garden, but no doubt the human–animal relationship closely mirrored our relationships with our pets today. There was probably a lot of playing between them, and the garden was filled with happiness and harmony.

Again, it is an intriguing possibility that verbal communication may have been possible. If that ability was in place, I am certain that animals will have that ability restored in the future, because whatever was part of the original plan will be made to be again. God is immutable. He never changes. I will expound on that thought in a moment, but for now I think it best to return to the question at hand, "What is life?"

At the risk of sounding a little far Eastern in my theology (and I assure you that I am not of those persuasions in even a small way), I want readers to know that there are several levels of life; or rather, several conscious states of life. Now that I see it in print, it does sound a little Eastern in philosophy, but I assure you that it is not intended to give any credence to anything but Bible tenets. If you hear me out, I believe you will agree.

If you take a moment to really think about it, there are definite differences between the various life forms found on, in, and under our world. I am not speaking of the different shapes, colors, and habits, of the various creatures, but rather the levels of awareness and intellectual abilities of different life groups.

Let me look at each of the groups in some depth to help you understand what I mean. While there may be some insignificant overlap between these levels of awareness that I will define, the distinguishing borders that separate one group from the others are very well defined. These levels, discussed in detail below, are sure to draw criticism from those who do not share my view. However, I must remain faithful to the facts of science and the teachings of the Bible.

Here then is the structure of nonmicroscopic life on our planet as I understand it. Again, I am not going to go into technical detail. I merely want to provide a brief overview of each level of life and qualify why they are higher or lower in the scale of consciousness.

PLANTS

I think any rational person would agree that plant life is a lower level of life than that of people. It is arguably the lowest level of life on earth. In fact, the term *life* may be an overstatement. The Bible says quite clearly that "Life is in the blood." Plants do not contain blood as we define it. It seems that their level of consciousness, if they have consciousness at all, is limited to an awareness of themselves. More accurately, it is an awareness of their needs and more a chemical reaction than anything else.

I have heard people say that they talk to their plants and that the plants respond with better growth and health. I find that a very hard concept to accept. It is much rather the case that people who are conscientious enough to converse with their plants might just be the kind of folks who attend to those plants much more proactively than others. It is probable therefore, even likely, that this is the reason for the better growth and not the verbal encouragement.

There seems to be evidence that plants think—the way ivy climbs, carnivorous plants trap prey, and tropical flora commission their seeds to populate foreign shores. We all know that appearances can be deceiving, however. I submit that these actions are simply the plant's natural and involuntary reaction to external stimuli.

When plants turn toward sunlight or a Venus flytrap closes and secretes digestive juices, it is because certain sensory apparatus is stimulated. I once fed a wad of paper to a Venus flytrap plant and it tried to process the object until I forcibly removed it the next day. As far as prolific tropical plants are concerned, such as the mangrove, these plants drop seeds where they will as does any plant. Since mangroves grow in or near the ocean, when seeds fall, they are carried away by the tide and deposited wherever the prevailing wind and current take them. How preposterous to imagine that mangroves might understand currents and tides. In spite of all that, let us avoid contention on the subject by assuming that plants do indeed possess life. Obviously, they grow and reproduce, so in some sense of the word, they are alive. But is this a conscious life?

The best way to explain my point about different levels of consciousness is to offer that:

- Plants have bodies.
- Animals have bodies and souls.
- Human beings have bodies, souls, and spirits.

Before we proceed any further, take a moment to understand this word *soul* in the context I am using it. *Soul* is translated from the Hebrew word *nephesh* over 100 times in the Old Testament. It is also used in the New Testament several dozen times as *psuche*. In ancient Greek and Hebrew, punctuation was usually absent from texts, so one had to rely upon the context in which the word was used. Many variances were possible, and it was difficult to interpret the meaning in the use unless you really rolled your sleeves up and spent time researching every word.

To give you an example of the vast application of these words, some of the translated words for *soul* are *breath, body, creature, desire, appetite, lust,* and *mind,* to name just a few. Again, application depends upon contextual use. To further exacerbate the problem of application, often people who use the word *soul* are just plain lazy and do no research before using the word in some new context. Thus, they use it inappropriately. They prefer to pass along what someone else has written or said without checking the interpretation themselves.

As a consequence, there is much controversy when the word is used. Especially exasperating is when someone misuses the word and then tries to correct someone who uses it correctly. In my work of helping people who contact me with their grief, writing articles on pet loss, or serving as guest author in an Internet chat room, I am occasionally confronted by alleged "Bible scholars" who want to call me on the carpet for my use of the word. Invariably, they try to give me a quick lesson in Greek or Hebrew. Believe it or not, I have even had people try to correct me by using Latin interpretations, when Latin was not a Bible language.

Admittedly, I am not an expert in Greek or Hebrew. I have

taken courses and can navigate my way through these languages in study, but I am far from being proficient. Also, I do not consider myself a Bible scholar. I do not think anyone is. I consider myself extremely knowledgeable in scripture, having several New Testament books and perhaps 10,000 verses memorized, but who truly can be a "scholar" in the infinite things and thoughts of God? At best, we remain ever students at His holy feet.

I do not want to take time to argue the fine points of interpreting the word *soul*. I completely understand the confusion people experience because of the many uses in scripture. Instead, in order to avoid any controversy in my use of the word, I am going to try an approach that I think all should be able to agree upon.

I know we have gone over this concept elsewhere in this book, but it does not hurt to revisit it to ensure that it is completely understood. Grasping this truth is foundational to understanding why animals are important to their creator and why he provides for them.

ANIMALS

The words *soul* and *spirit* are sometimes used interchangeably by people. Indeed, there are similarities, but there are distinct differences as well. The word used for soul, despite many variances, generally refers to your "life" or "essence." In other words, we do not have a soul, but we are a soul, or we are a life. In this sense, animals are the same as us. We both have a soul or life.

The word *spirit* is closely related, but very much different. The soul is who we are. It is our consciousness. It is "us." The spirit gives us a consciousness of God and alerts us to our need for Him. It sets us apart from animals. Animals have no need for God in the matters of redemption and reconciliation. They are innocent creatures.

When people use the word soul, almost without exception they are referring to that part of us that needs redemption. How many times have we seen in a movie where someone "sold their soul to the devil"? They actually mean that they sold their "God consciousness."

It is a misuse of the word, but one that has unfortunately been adopted into our accepted vocabulary. I want readers to know that when I refer to the word soul I am actually saying "life" or "life force." I am not speaking of the spirit. Rather, I am trying to illustrate the difference between animals and humans by showing that both have a "soul" or "life," but only humans have a spirit or "God consciousness."

This does not mean that animals are not loved by God, nor does it mean they are not provided for by Him. It is my opinion that animals will have their awareness of God awakened at the appropriate time in the future. There is no need for that now and it really is not an important point of discussion.

Animals are innocents. They have no sin and are not in need of redemption.

So many so-called scholars try to point out that animals have no hope of eternity because they have no redeemable soul. Bunk! Again, it is a misuse of the word. They really mean spirit. Either way, they are wrong.

Animals are innocents. They have no sin and are not in need of redemption. If we apply the flawed logic that since they have no soul (in the sense they are using the word) and cannot be in heaven, then we are going to have to kick out all the other beasts that are there, because they also have no need for redemption, either. And we cannot stop there. The angels also have to go, for they are not partakers in salvation. For that matter, God the Father is not in need of redemption. Would they deny Him a place in His own kingdom? How foolish.

In Job 12:10 we are told "in whose hands is the soul of every living thing." Obviously this word is inclusive of all things living. It does not differentiate. ALL are in God's hands. It does not say they are in His hands temporarily. It does not give a time limit at all. God is constant and eternal and whatever is in His hands is also eternal. Shall something die in the life-giving hands of God?

What does this tell us? Do we need to dig deeply to discover its meaning and intent as some "scholars" suppose. Does God hide things so that they are difficult to understand? The answer is an absolute and unqualified "no." God writes simply so we can understand. He simply says that the "life" or "life force" of every living thing is in His hands or under His control. This passage does not address the redeemable creature, but rather the life or consciousness of living things in general.

It is in this sense, then, that I assert that animals have a soul. I realize that I am discussing this in the section set aside for plants, but it was necessary to make this distinction now to assist us in framing the next category of awareness properly.

HUMANS

Human beings are at a higher level of life, greater in dimension than that of animals. Like plants and animals, we have a body that gives us self-awareness. This self-awareness is superior to both plants and animals in many ways, as we are able to better ourselves, achieve, and accomplish.

We have a soul or mind that is without question superior to any animal. It gives us an awareness of ourselves, as well as an awareness of other human beings, animals, and our surroundings in the physical world. However, it reaches beyond the apprehension of animals in that we look to the stars beyond as our realm of physical awareness. Animals do not.

Then, unique to humans, we have a spirit, which gives us an awareness of the supernatural and the unknown. Humans alone possess the capacity to perceive God, to worship an unseen deity, and to think and plan for life beyond this physical life.

I understand that there exists a general consensus that animals have a supernatural perception. We have all grown up under the assumption that animals have some sort of sixth sense. And truthfully, sometimes it appears they do. We hear tales of dogs seeing ghosts or other apparitions that we cannot see ourselves, of their hair standing up on their backs for no apparent reason, of horses stampeding out of their stalls or barns before an earthquake occurs, and countless other stories of that genre.

As a lad growing up in Hawaii, I remember well a story told to me by my brother-in-law. He told me how he and some of his friends had been out pig hunting in the mountains in the region of Oahu where the first wave of Japanese fighter planes came through in their attack on Pearl Harbor.

He continued with the story, telling me that as they came upon a grove of trees, their dogs stopped and howled at something that the men could not see. My brother-in-law swore that there was nothing to be seen . . . that there was nothing obstructing their view in the direction the dogs were looking.

The story gets a little nauseating here. I apologize for what I share with you next, but it is necessary for you to understand the story. The men, observing old Hawaiian folklore, took the maka pia pia (Hawaiian words for the "yuk" that collects in the corner of an eye) from their dog's eyes and wiped it in their own eyes. This, according to legend, allowed them to see what the dogs saw. And what they say they saw was a giant "ghost pig." Not just a ghost pig, but a giant one at that.

When I hear stories like this, I have to say, "Pass the bread, the baloney has already been around." I do not mean to disrespect my brother-in-law, but rather emphasize how people sensationalize the natural abilities of animals and assign a supernatural sense to them that they simply do not possess.

As a person who spends a lot of time in the wild and around animals, I can tell you that it certainly does appear that animals possess some sort of special sense. I believe there is another explanation, however. Isn't it more likely that their ability to sense impending earthquakes and their reaction to things that seem to not be there can be credited to their very keen senses of smell, hearing, and sight?

Animals have better senses than humans (and sometimes just plain better sense, too).

In other words, a horse running in panic several moments before we feel a quake is really a reaction to the horse's keen sense of hearing rather than some extrasensory perception. Because our hearing is inferior, we cannot hear the rumbling deep in the earth as readily as the horse.

Animals have better senses than humans (and sometimes just plain better sense, too). I think that it would surprise you to know just how much superior to our sense of smell is the dog's. Before I performed some research on the subject, I would have thought that a dog's sense of smell was perhaps five times better than the average human's. I could even probably have believed it was ten times more efficient. In fact, to my surprise, I learned that most household dogs have a sense of smell 30,000 times better than humans.

To put that in terms that provide more impact, let's say you entered a house where someone wearing perfume had just been visiting. The person had already left, but there was a faint wisp of perfume hanging in the air. You picked up on the sweet bouquet because there were still thousands of perfume particles in the air.

A week later, you have an opportunity to visit the house again and there is absolutely no trace of the perfume. The number of particles remaining in the air is almost zero, and you cannot detect even a whiff. But your dog can still smell the perfume.

If that gap in abilities is not enough to stagger you, try this . . . it is reported that bloodhounds, which are bred and used by design for searching by smell, have nearly three times the ability of smell than the average household dog possesses. A bloodhound's sense of smell is 80,000 times greater than yours and mine.

Conceivably, a bloodhound could sniff at a golf ball at a driving range for, say, two seconds, the ball hit out into the range among thousands of other golf balls, the dog released to find it, and successfully find that one ball without error. Sound too easy? Then try this remarkable true story on for size.

A young girl was abducted by a stranger in a van, driven about twelve miles away, and held captive in the van on a deserted road. It was later learned that the van did not stop once while traveling from the point of abduction to the deserted road twelve miles away.

Several hours after the abduction, the local authorities gave their bloodhound a piece of the child's clothing for reference and put the dog on the trail. It took several more hours, but the dog led police on foot down the same twelve miles of highway transited by the van, off the same exit ramp, and down the same deserted road. The bloodhound led them right to the van and the victim was rescued unharmed.

The handler estimated that the scent of the girl coming out of the van while passing at a normal rate of speed was perhaps

one part in several billion, which means it was almost indistin-
guishable. Yet, the animal picked it up and sorted it out from all
the other airborne odors, including the exhausts of all the thousands of vehicles that had passed by during the several hours of
searching.

Was it some sort of sixth sense the dog was employing? No,
it was not. He just possessed and employed far superior equipment than we humans have.

Humans, on the other hand, do possess a sixth sense of sorts.
Like animals, the average human being has the basic five senses.
Ours are not as sharp as those of animals, but they are more than
adequate and give us the wherewithal to operate and exist within
the physical confines of our world. Unlike the animals, however,
we have an additional ability to perceive or sense something
beyond the physical limits of our world. I have labeled this sense
SONG, which is simply an acronym for our ability to "sense our
need of God." Animals lack this ability, probably because they
do not need it. They are innocent creatures who have a standing
with God from their creation. They need no redemption or reconciliation.

I could be wrong, but I just do not see an awareness of God
in animals. Please do not misconstrue my words to mean that
they do not have a relationship with him, for he tells us that they
do. They apparently just do not seem to be aware of it at the
present. For instance, you will see birds building a nest, but never
a temple. You will see beavers building a dam, but never an altar.
Someone might teach a dog the "trick" of folding their paws and
bowing their head, but this does not qualify as praying and their
incentive is a treat rather than worship.

Humans alone have this awareness of God. Admittedly, there are those individuals who no longer recognize it, but that is their choice or the result of a hard, sinful lifestyle. They, like every person ever to live, once were aware of their SONG, but have cast aside the need they felt or purposely ignored it.

Those folks are few. It may seem sometimes like atheists run rampant in our country and world, but the numbers favor those who believe in some sort of supernatural deity. In every culture, even where the populace is oppressed and human rights appear to be nonexistent, where religious beliefs are forbidden, the sense lives on. It is something placed inside each of us by our creator.

Our SONG sets us apart from the animals and confounds the evolutionists (because even they feel that need inside themselves). You can believe what you will, but not one of us can honestly deny that sense in our heart and mind that someone is out there watching us, that everything is just too perfect to have just happened.

As I stated earlier, the Bible says that life is in the blood, or, to put it in other words, blood is needed to sustain the life of our body. The essentialness of its life-sustaining properties should not need validation. Every person in control of their faculties has demonstrated that they subscribe to this ideal when they react to a simple cut. Let anyone accidentally break the thin layer of epidermis that holds back their blood, and their immediate and total attention is focused on closing the breech, to the exclusion of almost everything else. Few matters take higher precedence with us than preserving our blood, because we know that when it runs out, so does our life.

How the entire mechanism of our circulatory system works and how that blood affects and effects life, who can say with certainty. Science can break down the parts and say, "It works and here is why," but they are looking at the result rather than the cause.

It is so much more complicated than that. Science can tell us everything about the parts of the blood, but when it comes to explaining how it is that our life is somehow in the blood, not many scientists step forward to speak. The only sure position is to acknowledge that life is of, from and in God, just like His word says. He wills it and He alone sustains it.

In a sense then (and this is where I hope you allow me some latitude and do not misconstrue my comments to be influenced by Eastern philosophy), God is life. When I consider all the facts of the preceding paragraphs, I must conclude that God is not only the source of life, but, since He alone has the power to make it, to control it, and to sustain it, He is effectively life himself.

He is the "life force," if you will. He existed before anyone or anything else alive existed. The record He gave us of the beginning of life states clearly that "He breathed life" into us. Hence, whatever life we have, it originated with God and nowhere else, especially not in a swamp (for even the swamp did not exist).

God is original life. The fact that life is now reproduced automatically and naturally does not diminish the fact that life exists because He wills and allows it to. To put it in the real context that I want to convey, God is life and we are sort of "little chips" of His life. I hope that makes sense to you, because I have overtasked my mind (you know, the one I previously claimed was so much superior to that of animals) searching for the best way to explain it. I want to say it more clearly, but that is going to have to suffice.

If you are still on board and haven't jumped ship on me yet, I need to sum up all I have said to make my point absolutely clear about what life is. In light of the fact that God is life and all life stems from Him, it only makes sense for us to conclude that irrespective of what happens to a living creature on this earth, the life or spirit of that creature can never and will never end. It is connected to the eternal God.

And as I search the scripture, God never created a temporal creature. Even Satan, great embodiment of evil that he is, will live forever and not be annihilated or extinguished. It is true that he will live in the judgment God has already pronounced upon him and never see heaven, but he will live on.

How presumptuous for men (and women) to think that God would spare an evil being like Satan from annihilation, but visit it upon such innocent and wonderful creatures as animals. That is not God's way. That principle is foreign to the Word of God. He did not create just to destroy.

If you are still with me, I need just a bit more latitude to bring these thoughts home. While it is my strong conviction that all life is in God's hands, and therefore cannot and will not end, equally strong is my conviction that there is a very big difference between animal and human life in regards to eternity.

For human beings, we all know, to varying degrees, that eternal rest and co-existence with God depends upon reconciliation through the savior He provided (it is His plan, not mine—it is from His Book). Many will enjoy that rest and fellowship as believers, while many others, we are told, will spend their eternal life in a place not quite as restful. The record of God's reconciliatory act can be believed or rejected. The choice is up to the individual.

If my stating that offends you, I am truly sorry. However, I can no more shade the truth to that than I can to any other of the truths I have shared with you in this book. Truth is truth whether we personally believe it or not. God gives a very easy to understand plan for reconciliation with Him in His word. The reason I bring this up at all is because there exists a spiritual quandary regarding animal and human afterlife, and if I did not make an effort to specifically point it out, some might miss it altogether.

Animals have no need for redemption, as I have already shown. It follows that they are, therefore, not subject to judgment in any sense of the word. Their eternity is sure. To see that in God's word is thrilling to my heart.

Conversely, people are in need of reconciliation. Our eternity is sure, but our destination may not be. Therein is the quandary. I can affirm that animals are safe and their future sure, but I do not want anyone thinking I can give them the same assurance for themselves. I do not have that authority. Nor would I be so presumptuous. That is an individual responsibility between each person and God. Many try to meet God on their terms, but the truth is, He demands we meet Him on his terms, coming to Him through his son (John 14:6).

I do not know how better to state that. I tried to be as inoffensive and unassuming as I could be. Some think I should say nothing at all, but that is not an option. What kind of a person would I be to bring hope and comfort to someone about their departed pet and not share with them the whole truth?

Chapter 5

THE MILLENNIUM

Before you decide to flip past this chapter, let me assure you that I am not going to burden you with lots of scripture. I understand that there is good probability that some readers do not share my love for the scriptures or my same faith in the Lord. I know that this would cause you to have a low tolerance level for someone quoting a lot of scripture, so I will refrain from doing so.

You will have to allow me some latitude, however, in order for me to complete my case on animal afterlife. This "millennium," or 1,000-year period, provides pertinent insight into the world and lives of animals that I do not think we can ignore. As there is only one source that talks about this last period of time before cataclysmic, eschatological events take place that will change our earth forever, I need to make several references to the information it offers.

Both the Old Testament and the New Testament make reference to this greatly anticipated period of Jesus' earthly reign (this is where the term "King of Kings" actually applies in scripture and history). After this 1,000 years of the theocracy he establishes, he destroys the old earth and heaven (atmosphere around the earth and what we call outer space) and creates the new earth. It would be so easy for me to get sidetracked here to go into greater detail about these events, but I will restrain myself from doing so and address only the things that apply to our study.

Paraphrasing some of the scriptural insights, the Bible tells us "The wolf shall dwell with the lamb, the leopard with the kid, the cow with the bear, their young ones shall lay down together and the lion shall eat straw like the ox."

Clearly, there will no longer be predator and prey. Moreover, there shall no longer be a schism between the animal and human world. Again, scripture says of the previously wild beasts, "and a child shall lead them" and "a child shall put his hand on the hole of the asp and the den of the cockatrice" (legendary offspring of a chicken and serpent in ancient Europe, more currently and correctly translated to be an adder).

The implication is unmistakable. During this period, animals will return to their first and intended estate of companion. They will not be carnivorous and we will have no need to fear them, or they us. There will no longer be wild beasts. Rather, all shall be domesticated. It appears that this will prevail throughout the animal kingdom, among mammals, reptiles, and birds.

Even more profound, they, and humans, shall live without death for the entire 1,000-year period. Since all living things will be herbivorous during this period, a great demand will be placed on the plant kingdom, already significantly decimated by the cataclysmic events foretold in scripture. I have to assume that since life will be prolonged, and the population increasing rapidly without natural attrition, conditions for growth of vegetation will be changed to produce optimal crops during this period. In fact, one might reason that since God will re-establish animals and people in their original relationship, He might well re-establish the original garden conditions, but on a much larger scale.

Imagine the wonder of no death, no unrest, no environmental disasters, no drought or flood, but rather harmony in nature and an incorruptible theocracy where perfect and pure judgments are rendered. It shall be a grand time.

Now then, in this picture of eternity we call the millennium, we have a reconfirmation of God's original plan for the life He created. After the millennium, there is nothing left to happen in our present universe. That is not to say that everything ends. Quite the contrary is true. We are told that this signifies the beginning of eternity for the life God created. We just are not told what happens after the universe we occupied for so long comes to an end.

A lot of very big things happen during this last thousand years, but once it is over, it is over, and those things are never experienced again. We enter the realm that is without time, the place (for lack of a better word) called "eternity." This is where God has always existed and now we become a part of it. Again, we are not told what will happen specifically, but we are told that all His creatures will enjoy this new relationship and life with their creator.

The animals, in confirmation of God's original plan for them, have been changed back to their original state during the millennium. They live without death or fear, the way God had originally planned for them to be. This is not a change, per se, but a change back. The original plan, as we noted earlier, was interrupted temporarily by man, and not by God's will or desire.

It would appear then that God's efforts of reconciliation of mankind to himself have come full circle since the fall. Faith will have been replaced with sight. In other words, mankind's former position with God will have been restored and everything set right again, the way it was intended. Believers will be with God. So, too, the evidence indicates, His original plan for animals has also come full circle, and they are once again as they were intended.

I think I have built a solid case. However, let me offer some additional thoughts for you to consider. As usual, no individual thought is enough to convince, but the evidence adds up to an overwhelming proof that God does care about more than just us humans.

Creatures we now refer to as animals were put in the garden to be with mankind. They were created before we were created. They were a forethought, not an afterthought. They were and remain important. God did not make them temporary creatures, but intended rather that they should live forever. Nothing has been written to suggest that God has changed His mind.

When the earth was destroyed by flood (by the way, almost every ancient culture historically references a worldwide flood), God preserved the animals along with mankind. When the water subsided, God made a covenant with Noah to never destroy the earth again by flood. God extended this covenant to the animals. Obviously, God's lesser creatures (those not made in His image) are indeed important to Him.

There is more. When Jesus was born, who did God the Father have present, people or animals? Of course Mary and Joseph had to be there, but there were no other people at the birth. Other people came later, but they were not at the birth. Yet, present were many from the animal kingdom. I will offer a more in-depth explanation of this in the upcoming sequel, but suffice it to say here that God found it acceptable for His son to be born in the presence of His innocent creatures.

Another momentous example of God's pleasure with His creatures is seen in the account of Jesus' fasting in the wilderness. We are told so very little about this period of Jesus' life, but what we are told is significant. Having retired away from his followers, to fast in the wilderness for forty days, it is offered that he spent the time with the wild beasts.

How interesting is it that Jesus chose to dwell among his creatures during this very solemn time of his ministry? How exciting to see the importance of animals in so many major historical events.

When we couple these stand-alone examples of God's comfortableness with His creatures with the picture of tameness we are given of their millennial existence, certainly we must conclude that they are important to God. We must acknowledge that animals are in it for the long haul and not just hitching a ride through our earthly history.

One scripture I have to offer to cap off this chapter is found in Revelation 5:13. If you have believed nothing else I have said about the eternity of animals, let this passage grip you. Study it out and try your best to make it say something other than what I offer you below. I assure you that you will not be able to do so. It says:

And every creature which is in heaven, and on the
earth, and under the earth, and such as are in the
sea, and all that are in them, heard I saying,
blessing and honor, and glory, and power, be unto
him that sitteth upon the throne, and unto the lamb
for ever and ever.

What more proof do we need? God, who cannot lie and who does not make mistakes, records that every creature was heard to praise Him. In my mind, *every* is an all-inclusive term meaning "all." So *all* creatures is what John (the writer used to pen this book of Revelation) is referring to. Not part, not some, not many, not just those that existed at the time of John's writing, but *all* creatures.

It also said of every creature, "which is in heaven," indicating strongly that some animals had passed on but still lived. One might argue that this refers only to animals whose only life was in heaven, and that would not be out of context at all. But the rest of the verse seems to cover every conceivable place animals could be, whether dead or alive, and this cannot be explained away without deliberate misinterpretation.

Finally, again, the verse says, "and *all* that are in them." This leaves little room to question just how many animals this includes. An acquaintance of mine gave me the best definition of this word *all* that I have ever heard. He said "*all* means *all* and that is *all* *all* means." The intent seems clear and unchallengeable *All* creatures, animal or human, living or dead, are important to God and are eternal creatures.

John wrote that all creatures would one day worship and praise

God. This is one of the major themes of the Bible, that God created mankind to worship and adore Him. We may get preoccupied with ourselves and our lives, but worship of God is what He created us for. Some may not like to hear that. It may not fit into their theology, or it may be offensive to them, but that does not mitigate the purpose of God. I would simply ask, "Who gave life to whom?" Then whose opinion really matters?

God's desire is that all of His creation worship and praise Him. That includes not only humans, who are made in His image, but the lesser creatures, which were made by His almighty hand. In fact, there are places in the scripture where God says even inanimate objects like the rocks will praise Him. So when God says "all," I think we should concede that He knew what He was saying and meant it.

God cares about His creation. He loves all the creatures made by His hand. He has made provision for them all. And I speak not only of earthly provision. The Lord tells us that He clothes the lilies of the field and keeps an eye on the sparrow. He oversees the lives of animals on this earth, directing their seasonal migrations and ensuring they have enough to eat. But He also cares about their eternity. Remember what we read in the Book of Job about the soul of every living thing being in His hands.

It is interesting to note that not only does the last book written in the Bible (Revelation) make reference to the eternity of animals, but also the book first written, Job (Genesis appears first in the Old Testament and is chronologically first in history, but Job was penned first). We see that this book gives testimony to the care God shows His creatures.

We can conclude that in God's entire revelation to mankind,

from beginning to end, He emphasizes the importance of animals, not to us, but to Him! Knowing that God is the only constant in our universe, given that He declares himself immutable, how can anyone be so presumptuous as to think God would change His mind about His animals?

Chapter 6

EXAMINING SCRIPTURE

In this chapter we are going to analyze scripture pertinent to our study. Hundreds of passages mention animals, but we will not look at all of them simply because they lend nothing to the topic at hand. Please do not be dismayed. There is an abundance of passages to consider and much to discuss.

I do not intend to bore you with word studies, linguistics, or the mechanics of transliterations. When I studied Greek, it was boring. It was boring every time, all the time. My guess is that it is still boring and I am not going to dwell on word meanings that you can study for yourself.

I am sure that would shock some of my mentors, but my sentiment is not meant to be a reflection on them personally. I am sure it was course content and not their teaching skills that drained my enthusiasm.

I certainly do not want to have that sort of effect on any of you, so expect me to keep this study simple. That is not meant to suggest that any of you are not able to follow. Rather, it is an admission that the topic is boring and I do not want it to adversely impact what I consider an interesting and important study.

So where I imagine you may want more depth to see what a word or phrase means, I will encourage you to study it on your own. Otherwise, you can be assured I have done the research myself, or at least reviewed and relied on the research of others who are much more capable than I in Greek and Hebrew. There should not be too many occasions where this is necessary since most of the scripture that follows is straightforward and easy to comprehend.

Let's begin with the acknowledgment that the word *animal* does not even appear in scripture. There are those who would call my credibility into question if I did not make this very elementary observation and I want to avoid such nit-picking.

Instead, the words *beast* or *creature* or the terms *every living thing* or *everything that has breath* are used. There are other lesser phrases as well, but they are too obscure for our use.

I have already explained in detail that God makes a radical distinction between animals and human beings. Nevertheless, sometimes people and animals are referred to in the collective, as we will note later in this text. This should in no way cause you to think that animals and humans are alike on any level as evolutionists would have you believe. We are not.

Evolution theory is not compatible with the Word of God, not even in its most accommodating (and therefore most dangerous) form of Theistic or Design Evolution. Theistic Evolution is discussed in great detail previously in this book, so we will not revisit it here. It is enough to say that the unproven theories of men cannot stand against the providential truths of God.

God made beasts one flesh and he made mankind another. We are different in being and in spirit. The Bible is a book for man, not for animals. But there is enough said about animals that we can safely draw some conclusions about them and see the big picture of God's plan for them.

The evidence shows that animals are a very important part of God's creation. I detest the "oh, it was only a dog mentality" of some people. Animals are creatures formed by the hands of Almighty God. That fact alone assigns an importance to them that transcends any ideas we may have.

When He had finished creating, the Bible tells us that He personally assessed *all* that He had made as being "very good." It is obvious that both creation and creature brought God pleasure. To minimize the importance of these creatures is to foster a view that is not biblical.

Animals have been present throughout history. In fact, they were here before man, if only for one day. They were in the Garden of Eden with Adam and Eve. God placed them there to be companions for Adam. He even gave Adam the privilege of naming them. There was complete harmony between man and animal in the Garden.

Animals have been the companions of mankind ever since. Our connection to them is undeniable. They were there at creation. They dwelled with us in the garden. When God judged the world and exacted His wrath with a deluge, He remembered the animals and had Noah build an ark to carry them in safety for the ten months the earth was flooded.

Animals are given the spotlight or special privilege in many places in scripture. For instance, they were present at the birth of the son of God in the manger. Not only were they there, but their presence was to the exclusion of people other than Mary, who you will agree had to be there, and Joseph, who needed to be there.

Was it really by chance that there was no room for Joseph and Mary in the inn, or did God purposely choose for his Holy Son to enter the world in the presence of innocent animals? It is only my opinion, and you can assign it whatever worth you please, but I lean toward the latter being the case.

The birth of his Son is not something I think God would have left to chance. The kingdom, province, and city where this great event would occur were prophesied long before it happened. Joseph was given instructions by an angel. God instilled in Caesar's heart to decree that all the world should be taxed and that everyone should return to their hometown. With all this attention to detail, it is hard to imagine that God would then just leave everything else to chance.

Undoubtedly, the Father chose this very stable as the place where Christ should be born. Here indeed he was born, with the only invited guests being the two people who needed to be there and the livestock who called the stable home.

You might say, "But what of the wise men and the shepherds; they were present at his birth, weren't they? All of the nativity scenes and Christmas plays show us that. Doesn't the Bible support that?"

Actually, no, it does not. In fact, it gives us a completely different picture. I would like to take a moment to address this common misconception. I know I will be wandering from the topic at hand a little, but I think you will find it interesting.

The assumption that the wise men and shepherds were present in the manger at the birth of Christ is unsupportable in scripture. We can quickly dismiss the notion that the shepherds were there, because in Luke, chapter 2, the angels speak to the shepherds, telling them that the event had already occurred. The shepherds responded to this announcement by saying:

> *Let us even go now and see this thing which has*
> *come to pass, which the Lord has made known*
> *unto us.*

Now let's discuss the wise men or magi. To begin, let me clear up a mathematical discrepancy that has always bothered me. Nowhere does the Bible say that there were three wise men. There may well have been, but I don't know. No one on this earth knows.

Given that the custom of that day was for people of means to travel with a large company for reasons of safety and adequate logistics, it is more likely that there were far more than three wise men. Some theologians estimate the number as high as forty, with scores or even hundreds of attending servants accompanying them.

What the Bible does say quantitatively, and no doubt where the discrepancy originates, is that there were three gifts offered (gold, frankincense, and myrrh). Since there are three gifts, people have believed that the gifts were the offering of three individuals.

The conclusion is understandable, but not a likely scenario. The evidence suggests that a greater company sought the Christ child. These were considered high-end gifts in those days and if there were a dozen magi, for instance, there were probably several gifts of gold, several gifts of frankincense, and several gifts of myrrh. If you have ever attended a wedding reception, you know how common duplicate gifts are.

Irrespective of how many magi there were, we can easily eliminate them from having been present at Christ's birth. At the same time that Jesus was being born in Bethlehem, Herod the king was making inquiry to these same wise men on the other side of the territory he ruled about where the birth should take place.

Communications between them was slow. There were no cell phones or e-mail. There were couriers. Couriers had to travel by foot or by beast. Chariots were not ordinarily used by couriers, but when they were, they were no faster than the beasts that drew them.

Moreover, these couriers had to take the longer, safer routes in their journeys to avoid being the victims of bandits. Several exchanges between Herod and the wise men were necessary and would take months to accomplish.

When the wise men told Herod where this blessed event would take place, he commissioned them to go to locate the child and to bring word back again to him. His intent was not to pay homage to this new "king" as he had falsely articulated to the wise men, but rather to find the Christ child and eliminate him. Herod saw Christ as a threat to his own authority.

There is much conjecture about where the wise men departed from, exactly when they actually departed, and how long was their journey. In fact, there are several conflicting opinions, all with equal merit.

It is important to note that each of the views have one thing in common: the magi began their journey in a province at least many months' journey from Bethlehem. Indeed, the evidence suggests that the communications with Herod, preparation for the journey, and the actual travel for such a large entourage took almost two years. Obviously, they could not have been witness to the birth of Christ.

How do we know that it took two years? In Matthew, chapter 2, verse 8, Herod refers not to the infant or babe, but to the "young child." Obviously, the birth of the Messiah had long been past. This is further supported by verse 9 where "young child" is again used instead of infant or babe. Finally, it is used yet again in verse 11, on the occasion of the wise men's arrival in Bethlehem. We are told:

> *And when they were come into the house, they saw*
> *the young child with Mary his mother.*

Their journey had been an extended undertaking. Jesus was no longer an infant, but a toddler. The verse also uses the word "house," not manger. Joseph and Mary had long since left the stable and established a residence. Whatever the reason: whether it was the time it took for Herod and the wise men to communicate back and forth through couriers, a delayed departure, or a long journey, it is certain the wise men were not present at the birth of Jesus.

We are told in verse 12 that the wise men were warned of God that they should not return to Herod. Why? It was because Herod determined evil against the Christ Child. We know this is true by the testimony of verse 16, where Herod ordered the slaying of all the children in Bethlehem under the age of two.

That Herod chose the age of two is no accident. It had been just under two years since the birth of Jesus and Herod wanted to make sure that the child did not escape. By slaughtering all the male children two years old and younger, he hoped to ensure that Jesus would be among them.

Historical evidence bears out this horrific slaughter. In the late 1970s a mass grave containing the bones of approximately seventy-five male children under the age of two was discovered in Bethlehem, an infamous testament to the vanity and wickedness of Herod.

There you have the actual record of the nativity. I apologize for the short detour from our study. I simply wanted to give an example of how animals are very important to God and how they often fit into His purposes. I think it is significant that God preferred the presence of innocent animals rather than people at His son's birth.

Not only were animals present at Christ's birth, but later, during Christ's forty days in the wilderness, it was the animals that enjoyed his company, not people. Scripture tells us that Jesus spent his time of fasting and praying among the wild beasts.

I am tempted to claim great significance to this, but it would be purely speculative on my part, so I will restrain myself from doing so at this point. Still, it is clearly relevant that the Lord is comfortable around his lesser creatures, that he enjoys them. When we look at the rest of scriptural evidence, that relevance will take on greater significance.

Moving on, we also see animals in the millennium, which, according to scripture, is the last 1,000-year period of this earth. This is a time when Jesus returns to the earth to set up his kingdom. During this time, animals are changed to be as they were in the Garden of Eden. They will again be tame.

There will be no predator or prey. Animals will no longer be carnivorous, but herbivorous, eating hay and other vegetation as they live in harmony with each other and with mankind. Scripture speaks of the lion walking with the lamb with no conflict or danger, the child playing with a venomous serpent, and the animals being completely tame. They are as God originally intended for them to be. God did not change His mind about them and restores them to their original state.

That God is immutable is a foundational point to the conclusions drawn here. He changes not. This fact cannot be disputed. Accordingly, since God never changes we can and must conclude that all He providentially said would be, will indeed be.

God's original plan was that man and animal would live forever without death. His immutability, by definition, ensures that this plan has not changed and both remain under the umbrella of His providence. Animals may suffer in this life and succumb to physical death as a result of what mankind did in the garden, but their eternal "essences" are preserved in God, as noted earlier.

Now then, we have seen the important role that animals have played throughout history. They helped us hunt for food, helped lead us with their superior senses, carried our burdens, and served in the role of companion. They were there at every important milestone of our past and will be there at important milestones in the future. Man and animal are a matched set, intended to co-exist.

Why then would we doubt that, like us, they have eternal essences? Why do some deny them a part in God's eternal plan? There is overwhelming evidence in scripture that they are eternal beings and not even a hint that they are not. We should be able to rest our case on this one thought alone, that God's plans never change. Unfortunately, for some that is not enough.

So we will look at more convincing evidence. As we do, I pause to remind you that the Bible is the sole source and resource for my work and this author believes with his heart that every word of scripture is given by the providence and inspiration of God. You will find no footnotes or appendixes giving credit to any person or organization other than the Lord for the ideas and conclusions set forth in this book, because no other source was used.

Let us look at the scriptural support for my contention that animals are extremely important to God, that they are an intricate part of His creation and remain forever under His watchful eye. I hope that you have a Bible handy, because you may want to take a contextual look at the passages surrounding the scripture I will discuss to satisfy yourself that I am representing the intent of what has been written.

Passages will be discussed in no particular order, except that I will attempt to remain topical in presentation, but that will not always be possible, so I beg your indulgence. The format for this section of the chapter will be:

- I will give the verse reference.
- I will give the verse in extract form.

🐾 I may provide emphasis by italicizing a word(s).

🐾 I will provide commentary if needed or let it stand alone if self-explanatory.

Let us begin.

Psalm 36:6

> *Thy righteousness is like the great mountains; thy judgments are a great deep: O LORD, thou preservest man and beast*

While some would like to elevate the word *preservest* to a spiritual level, this verse speaks only to earthly existence. It addresses God's providential care over animals, as well as people. That is an important revelation, however, because once again, God's immutability comes into focus.

If God has an earthly care for His animals, does it make sense that He suddenly changes His mind when they pass from this earth and allows them to simply cease to exist? Can God suddenly change the way He feels?

The answer to both questions of course is "no." God is unchangeable. Another way to state this is to say that God is consistent. He is the only true constant in our universe. If He cares for His creatures now, He cares for them forever. They belong to Him and when He speaks of them in scripture, there is a connotation of permanence to this declaration of ownership, as evidenced in the following passage.

Psalm 50:10–12

> For every beast of the forest is mine, and the cattle
> upon a thousand hills. I know all the fowls of the
> mountains: and the wild beasts of the field are
> mine. If I were hungry, I would not tell thee: for
> the world is mine, and the fullness thereof.

Psalm 150:6

> Let every thing that hath breath praise the Lord.

There are many, many texts in scripture that speak of the creature praising the creator. There are even instances where God commands inanimate objects like stones to praise him. As evidenced by the first two commandments, God is a jealous God who desires praise from His creation. We are told that there are beasts around His throne that praise Him day and night. It is clear that His desire is for animals to praise Him for all eternity as well as people and angels.

Job 12:10

> In whose hand is the soul of every living thing.

This is a very profound passage. The initial, face-value perception is that God is speaking of all creatures, human and animal. The considered, in-depth study of the statement supports the initial perception. It is speaking of both.

The word *soul* is used in over twenty different ways in the Bible. Invariably, when people come across this word in scripture, they automatically associate it with redemption. As a consequence, no distinction is made in the different applications.

This explains why some people readily balk at the idea that animals have souls. In their minds, to acknowledge that animals have a soul is tantamount to saying animals can be redeemed. Clearly, this is not what scripture teaches. The gospel message is not for animals. They are not in need of redemption. The gospel is exclusively for people; it is a reconciliatory outreach from God to mankind.

However, to allow this truth to cause one to draw the conclusion that animals therefore cannot have souls is to visit a gross injustice on scripture. Again, there are many applications to this word that have nothing to do with redemption.

An example of this is the Hebrew word *nephesh* (soul). This word appears many times in scripture and is used to describe both the essence of man and animals. It does not make a distinction between the two and it does not delve into salvation in its application. Rather, it addresses the consciousness.

This passage in Job addresses providential care. A clearer meaning of this verse would be "in whose hand is the *life* or *essence* of every living thing . . ." God is speaking of that part of humans and animals that contains or houses the life that He has given to them; that part that departs the body when the body expires.

When we mesh this thought in Job with Romans, chapter 8, and Revelation, 5:9–13, to name a few corresponding passages, the meaning is clear. The life or essence of every living thing is in the eternal care of the one who created that life.

However, this word in Job indicates an even deeper thought for us to consider. We often think of ourselves as a flesh-and-blood body with a soul. This is not so according to scripture. In keeping with the absolute intent of this word, we are souls that have been placed in flesh-and-blood bodies. The distinction is subtle, but it is immense in effect. This is our essence, that we are a soul, not a body. The body is temporal, but the soul eternal.

Since the same word is used for people and animals, this truth applies to animals as well. They are not creatures with souls, but are eternal souls given temporary bodies. So when we refer to their soul, we are merely acknowledging that animals have essence and that this essence is eternal in nature. They are innocent creatures whose souls are safe in the hand of their creator, and there can be no safer place to be than in the hands of God.

Genesis 9:9–12, 15

> *And I, behold, I establish my covenant with you,*
> *and with your seed after you; and with every living*
> *creature that is with you, of the fowl, of the cattle,*
> *and of every beast of the earth with you; from all*
> *that go out of the ark, to every beast of the earth.*
> *And I will establish my covenant with you; neither*
> *shall all flesh be cut off any more by the waters of*
> *a flood. . . . And I will remember my covenant,*
> *which is between me and you and every living*
> *creature of all flesh.*

Who can argue the fact that God made animals party to the peace covenant He was making with mankind. This should serve to convince you that an eternal relationship exists between God and animals. God's covenants are always eternal. Besides, what purpose would making a covenant with animals serve if their consciousness was for this world only?

God's care for his creatures is a testament to both His love and immutability. God has never changed His mind about man or animal. His love for both is eternal and so is His plan. His original plan was for them to live forever. Despite the fall of Adam and Eve and the advent of physical death because of sin, God will bring to pass His plan of eternal life for all. His love demands it and His immutability ensures it.

Revelation 5:13

And every creature which is in heaven, and on the earth, and under the earth, and such as are in the sea, and all that are in them, heard I saying, Blessing, and honor, and glory, and power, be unto him that sitteth upon the throne and unto the Lamb (Jesus) for ever and ever.

There will be some who will say that this word *creature* speaks of people only, but that is not so. When you consider the words *and all that are in them,* especially in light of the other scripture we have looked at, there can be no doubt but that God is speaking again of His entire creation, every creature, not just a select few.

There are many references to "creatures" and "beasts" in heaven. We see the horsemen of the Book of the Revelation and the creatures that are around the throne of God praising him, to name a few. Jesus himself will return to earth for his church on a horse. The evidence of animals in heaven is strong and compelling.

However, even if there was no reference, and even if after I arrived in heaven myself I saw no evidence of animals, I would still be confident that God had provided for them somehow. I know this because, as I said earlier, God's plan was that they should live forever and God never changes his plans, for His plans are—like Him—perfect.

Ask yourself this question: If God exercises so much concern and care for animals in this life, what would cause Him to stop caring when they passed from this life? If He were capable of doing that, then He could just as easily change the way He feels about us. Thankfully, scripture tells us that God can never stop loving His creation. It is His nature to love what His hands have made.

The fact is that even those people God reluctantly gives up to hell will never be forgotten by Him, nor will He stop loving them. The Bible tells us that He will wipe away all of our tears so that we do not have continuing sorrow. Some speculate that this suggests He will wipe away our memories of those who missed heaven.

Whether that is so or not will not be known until it happens, but one thing is certain: God can never wipe His own memory away, for He is omniscient. It will undoubtedly break His heart for someone to miss heaven because they rejected His son, and I am sure He will shed tears for them for all eternity.

This will no doubt be ill received by some, but I submit to you that God will even feel remorse for the wicked Satan and his horde of demons. God created them. He loved them. They went bad, but that does not change the character of God. God loves.

The scripture doesn't say He has love, but rather that He *is* love. It is His nature to love. He loves all His creation and all its creatures and because of His immutability, He loves them for eternity.

If God continues to love even this wicked creature named Satan who has perpetrated so much evil in our world, is it so difficult to believe that He continues to love these wonderful and devoted personalities we call pets?

Genesis 1:24–25

> *And God said, Let the earth bring forth the living*
> *creature after his kind, cattle, and creeping thing,*
> *and beast of the earth after his kind and it was so.*
> *And God made the beast of the earth after his*
> *kind, and the cattle after their kind, and every*
> *thing that creepeth upon the earth after his kind:*
> *and God saw that it was good.*

Three points need attention here. First, we are told that the creatures were made "after their own kind." If this does not completely uproot the evolutionary tree, than no other argument will.

God said that He created it all and that all were made exactly as they are.

None have determined their own way through natural selection. None have evolved. How I fear for those who take issue with God over this. They would deny Him the credit for what He did and give that credit instead to some imaginary "Mother Nature."

Second, to repeat myself, God said of what He had made "that it was good." God made nothing bad. Nothing that God made needs to be re-engineered or evolved. Natural selection usurps the providence and ability of God to create the creatures as He wanted them to be. Evolution says it was not good and needed to be changed, updated, or made better.

Finally, God made these animals after their own kind. They were not made in his image, only mankind was. They will never turn into you or me.

I do not like being referred to as a mammal. I am not a mammal. I am not an animal. I am a man. None of my ancestors hung from a tree by their tail. Some may have hung by their necks, but never by their tails.

Genesis 1:30

> And to every beast of the earth, and to every fowl
> of the air, and to every thing that creepeth upon the
> earth, wherein there is life, I have given every green
> herb for meat: and it was so.

If any topic I mention in this book has the potential to open a can of worms, it will probably be this one, that God intended for all creatures to be vegetarians, including man. I have found people to be more opinionated on this subject of meat versus veggies than any other animal-associated topic. I have wisely decided to not take sides or answer questions about whether I am a vegetarian or not, because you just cannot please everyone.

For the record, vegetarianism was the plan in the beginning. When the fall occurred, when man rebelled against God and disobeyed Him, everything changed and flesh was added to the menu under the curse of sin. It was not God's will for this to be, it was part of the penalty we brought upon ourselves. Today, many people find the eating of meat offensive, but most do not.

Animal rights have finally become important issues in our society and I am happy for it. From local chain laws to national attention on using animals for testing, we are finally securing the respect that these creatures deserve.

The question of whether to eat meat or not has also become an animal rights' issue. Some organizations push for everyone to become vegetarians, and other organizations support the opposite view. The battle has raged for many decades and I suspect that it will continue for quite some time.

No matter what transpires here on earth regarding animals, whether it is right or wrong that they are a food source or that they are used for testing, God has not dismissed His concern and care for them. Someday, the books will be opened, there will be an accounting, and everything that was wrong will be made right.

God will have His way irrespective of who disagrees with Him and that will be that. That is about as far as I want to go on that subject for fear of pallets of mail arriving on my doorstep.

Genesis 3:1

Now the serpent was more subtle than any beast of the field which the Lord God had made.

The serpent here is commonly accepted to be Satan. Some people tell me it is not, but they have no support for that position. There can be no doubt of who the serpent was.

It is speculated by most Bible scholars that this serpent was not the typical serpent of today. The serpent in the garden they say, at least the one who headlines the story with Adam and Eve, did not crawl on its belly. Rather, it walked upright.

This train of thought comes from the curse recorded in verse 14 where God said the serpent would henceforth crawl on its belly, suggesting that it had not done so previously. The curse continues to this day. It has lasted a long time.

Perhaps part of the curse is the disdain people feel toward the serpent. Something like nine out of ten people have a fear or dislike for snakes. I am the one out of ten. I do not dislike them. In fact, I like them.

As a young child, I had a slightly older and considerably larger sister who used to pick on me quite regularly. When I discovered the reaction and respect I received from her after putting a snake down her back, I knew there had to be something good about them. And I have never lost my interest in them.

Now before you accuse me of being sympathetic to a satanic symbol of some sort, please remember Genesis 1:31 where God said of everything He had made, including the "creeping thing" that it was very good. God did not consider snakes "yukky." He made them with His hands and how does that old bumper sticker go? Oh yes—"God don't make no junk."

If that is not enough, read John 3:14, where it says:

And as Moses lifted up the serpent in the wilderness, even so must the Son of man be lifted up.

Briefly, in the Old Testament, God once judged Israel for their waywardness by sending fiery serpents among them. These serpents bit the people and they died. The people complained to Moses and he passed their complaint on to God. Moses was told by God to affix a brass serpent on a pole and to instruct the people that if someone was bitten by one of the serpents they should look to the brass serpent to be spared. This was a test of their faith. If they had faith in God, they looked. If they didn't, oh well!

In the book of John, God makes a comparison of this serpent on a pole to the crucifixion of his son, the Lord Jesus. The brass serpent was a type or picture of Jesus being nailed on the cross and lifted into the air. If anyone looks to Christ, they receive forgiveness and do not die a spiritual death. If anyone looked to the serpent, they received forgiveness and did not die. If God would make a comparison of a serpent to His son, I doubt that God thinks that snakes are evil.

Genesis, Chapter 7

This chapter is too lengthy to reproduce here, but I recommend you read it in its entirety. It is the account of the animals on the ark during the flood. There are some things that we have already covered, so I will not revisit them here. It is just a good foundational portion of scripture to see God's providence and care for His creatures.

I did want to share two questions with you, though, that most people never ask. There is no point in my mentioning them except to shine the spotlight once again on God's love and care for His creatures. The questions are:

- 🐾 How did two of all the animals from all over the earth arrive at where Noah had built the ark? Some had to cross oceans, some had to endure climates that they were not suited for, and so forth. How did they do it?
- 🐾 Similarly, after the flood, how did the animals get dispersed back to the regions where they are now exclusively found?

The Bible does not give us the answers, but there can be only one possible explanation. God had to have accomplished it, supernaturally. He brought the animals to where the ark was and after the waters receded He returned them back to where they had come from.

Genesis 9:1–3

And God blessed Noah and his sons, and said unto them, Be fruitful, and multiply, and replenish the earth. And the fear of you and the dread of you shall be upon every beast of the earth . . . into your hand are they delivered. Every moving thing that liveth shall be meat for you.

Here are some powerful words from God to Noah. As I said earlier, the curse was responsible for changing the menu for man and beast. But that is not the point being made here. In these verses we are told that the animals are delivered into our hands. We have dominion over them.

We have all seen the reaction of animals to humans. Even domestic animals, including our own pets, display a fear of us at times. It is an unfortunate by-product of the curse, but in no way should their fear and apprehension diminish our responsibilities to treat them well.

Numbers 20:11

And Moses lifted up his hand, and with his rod he smote the rock twice: and the water came out abundantly, and the congregation drank, and their beasts also.

God told Moses to give water to the people and to their beasts. This verse represents many, many verses that speak to the issue of God's care and concern for animals. Prior to the disobedience in the garden, God provided sustenance for both animals and people.

Now, after that infamous turn of events known as "the fall," the responsibilities were shared. God would provide for the wild creatures and man for those he domesticated. Even then, God displays His love for His creatures by giving men instructions for their care.

Since that time in the garden, there has emerged a new relationship between animals and people. In the new relationship animals are beasts of burden, working at the direction of man. Even in the capacity of family pet, animals serve people as guardians, herders, mousers, and so forth.

Regardless of this change in relationship, God still requires care be given to His animals when they are under our dominion. Moses knew this and ensured that he articulated that thought in the words God gave him to tell the people.

You may also want to visit Numbers 35:3, where God ensures that the people set aside grazing land for their animals. Throughout the Bible God takes a proactive role in ensuring that animals are not mistreated and that their needs are met.

Job 35:11

Who teacheth us more than the beast of the earth,
and maketh us wiser than the fowls of heaven?

Do not misinterpret this verse as giving credit to animals for being wiser or more intelligent than we are. The intent of Elihu's discourse to Job, the servant of God, was to show him that God is so righteous and wise that even nature and the natural order of the animal kingdom reflect his wisdom. When this passage is read in concert with Job 10:7–10, it teaches that we can learn much about God's providence through His creation.

His watch care over the animal kingdom speaks to His Lordship over nature. It dispels the thought that nature is an entity in and of itself and shows God's authority and control over all He has created.

Psalm 49:12–20

There are two portions of scripture that initially appear to cast doubt on animal afterlife. This is one of them. The other is in the book of Ecclesiastes (which we will discuss below). Please read the verses first and then come back to finish reading the commentary. This portion of scripture is extremely relevant, but too lengthy to reproduce here.

If you have read the verses as I asked, you probably are a little concerned about what you read. You will admit that it seems to say that men are not like the beasts that perish. Automatically you assume the passage speaks of a spiritual death since physically speaking, it is already common knowledge that men die just like the animals, and vice versa. This is a very good example of how the transposing of words from Greek and Hebrew can sometimes lose their meaning, requiring a little extra effort to discern the intent.

The key to understanding this portion of scripture would be to read verses 12, 16, 17, and 20 together to determine the topic, much like how you dissect a sentence to determine what the noun or pronoun is. Our inclination is to think these verses are addressing the fate of beasts, but in fact, the topic is the fate of men of riches and honor who lack understanding of God.

The lesson is that when they go to the grave, they are "like the beast that perishes," meaning they cannot take their honor or riches with them. They leave with nothing, just like the beasts that leave with nothing, because they had nothing in this life, except the fur or feathers on their backs and the providential care of God.

It is prudent to readers of the Bible that they identify what the key issue of a portion of scripture is. If you miss the emphasis, you can also miss the truth being expounded. There is no point being made in this portion of scripture concerning the eternity of animals and none should be read into it.

Psalm 73:22

So foolish was I, and ignorant: I was as a beast
before thee.

This scripture can only be interpreted one way, that beasts have no knowledge of God. It is not something bad, only factual. That animals do not possess an awareness of God in the same way mankind does, does not mean they are not provided for by Him.

Animals remain under God's providential and eternal care. He watches over them. He feeds them. He tells them when to fly south or north, when to migrate, and where to find the grazing grass during the migration. God's watch care is constant and sure over His creatures. They just are not aware of it.

Let me illustrate this point. I once sold a home and was happy with the modest profit I had made. I did not realize, however, that a considerable amount of escrow was due back to me. A few months after the sale of the home, a government agency contacted me to advise me that I had a refund in escrow coming to me if I would just complete a particular form.

Not only did I not know that I was due back escrow, but I did not even know that this agency existed. I was unaware of them and their charter. Despite my ignorance of their existence, they were watching out for me and I benefited from it.

The animals are ignorant of God's existence and His watch care over them while they are on this earth, but God continues to watch over them and provide for them.

Proverbs 12:10

A righteous man regardeth the life of his beast: but the tender mercies of the wicked are cruel.

Although all scripture is given for instruction and reproof, it is the Proverbs where we see an abundance of Godly wisdom given that we might apply to earthy circumstances. Each chapter of Proverbs is filled with many different witticisms and thoughts on various topics.

In this verse we are shown the contrast between righteousness and wickedness. God says it is a righteous act to regard (or care for) the life of our animals. Logic tells us that this means we should treat them well, care for their needs, and protect and provide for them.

As I study the Bible, I have learned that God would never ask us to be something that He himself is not. He wants us to care for our beasts because He cares for them.

He also would not lay behavioral foundation or pattern for something that would be of temporal use to us. In other words, if He tells us to care for our animals, embedding it into our core values of what is right and what is not, we can be sure that this is a virtue He intends for us to keep for all time.

God's attributes are eternal and never change. He does not reproduce them in us to be temporary, but eternal as well. It doesn't make sense that He would teach us a value that will not stand for all time and eternity, because that value emanates from His own eternal righteous character. Caring for animals is something that God wants us to do because it is something He does. And if God does something, it is right. If it is right now, it is right forever.

Ecclesiastes 3:18–21

> *I said in mine heart concerning the estate of the*
> *sons of men, that God might manifest them, and*
> *that they might see that they themselves are beasts.*
> *For that which befalleth the sons of men befalleth*
> *beasts; as the one dieth, so dieth the other; yea,*
> *they have all one breath; so that a man hath no*
> *pre-eminence above a beast: for all is vanity. All go*
> *unto one place; all are of the dust, and all turn to*

> *dust again. Who knoweth * the spirit of man that*
> *goeth upward, and the spirit of the beast that goeth*
> *downward to the earth?*

This is that second portion of scripture that I told you would present some difficulty. The last line would seem to indicate that the spirit of man goes "up" (meaning to heaven) and the spirit of the beast goes "down" (meaning to hell).

If this is so, we have nothing to celebrate, no hope that our "best friends" will have a part in the afterlife and our study has been in vain. We might as well close this book, grab our hankies, and go find a place to weep.

Not so fast! This is not at all what these verses are saying. The easy answer I could give you is that the translators erroneously omitted the word *whether* from the text (see the asterisk I implanted in the verse for proper positioning). Most new translations carry a footnote explaining this oversight.

An obvious question would be *How can that be—I thought the word was inspired?* Let me assure you that a mistake by a translator had no effect on inspiration. Inspiration was a one-time, never to be repeated, act of God to write through selected holy vessels (men) exactly what He wanted to write.

Translators merely took the Inspired Word that had already been delivered and translated it into other languages. An error in translation has no effect on inspiration, because inspiration was effected long before any translation was undertaken. However, translation of a text can effect "preservation" of scripture and that is why there are so many inferior translations today.

That said, you can see that the rendering of the verse is completely different when the omitted word is added. I don't know whether the omission was deliberate or not. It may have been, but people make mistakes and I suppose we need to give the translators the benefit of the doubt.

Let us assume that the verse includes the omitted word and now reads "who knows whether. . . ." This too poses a difficulty. With the word omitted, it is a bad fit because it would indicate that all men go "up," when we know that this is in direct contrast with what both Old and New Testaments teach (which might explain why some omitted the word in the first place).

With the word added, however, it suggests that a beast's spirit can go either way. In other words, animals somehow are able to determine their own destiny. This not only conflicts with other passages of scripture, but it circumvents the focus of this portion of scripture.

Solomon, in this book of Ecclesiastes, is writing on the vanity of life, in particular the life of men. It is absolutely wrong to think beasts are the focus of this passage. Solomon was merely showing that men and animals both return to dust and that proves that this life is vain. If anything, verse 14 of this chapter validates the fact that God's initial plan for men and animals will surely be brought to pass.

If we were to consider anything in this passage pertinent to our study of God's providence toward animals, we would focus on the word *spirit* in verse 21. This verse should silence the naysayer; it confirms that animals have spirits.

This revelation is huge, because the word *spirit* is used only in an eternal context in scripture. In other words, the spirit is not only our life-giving force now, but is also that part that lives on after this life.

This is remarkable evidence from God on the topic of animal afterlife. He tells us in a very straightforward and undeniable way that animals have spirits. In effect, they possess a "forever life." Since animals are not subject to judgment and consequently cannot and will not be put in hell, their spirits must go somewhere. The only other "somewhere" we are told about in scripture is that place where God lives, or heaven.

Since we already see animals around the throne, since we know that God's heaven is where His saints (anyone who places trust in Him) go, and since the angels who kept their first estate are there, it is a pretty safe assumption that animals will all be there, too. We only need to look to the Garden of Eden to see how well co-habitation works. There was complete harmony between God, man, and animal.

The next passage we look at will add credence to the above view. It discusses a period known as the Millennium, or the last thousand years on earth before God makes a new heaven and new earth. It is rather exciting to read what conditions will be like during this period.

Isaiah 11:6–8

The wolf also shall dwell with the lamb, and the
leopard shall lie down with the kid; and the calf
and the young lion, and the fatling together;
and the little child shall lead them. And the cow

> *and the bear shall feed; their young ones shall lie*
> *down together: and the lion shall eat straw like the*
> *ox. And the suckling child shall play on the hole of*
> *the asp, and the weaned child shall put his hand*
> *on the cockatrice den.*

This is an enormously encouraging portion of scripture. It shows a return of animals to their natural tame state, the way they were originally created to be. It is strong confirmation of what I said earlier concerning God's providential will for His creation, to wit: that despite our fall in Eden, God will bring His will to pass and animals will live forever.

These verses thrill me more than any of the others for they support my most basic contention that God never changes and that what He planned in the beginning, even though temporarily offset by mankind's disobedience, is not lost. He will bring His perfect will to pass.

Isaiah 43:20

> *The beast of the field shall honor me, the dragons*
> *and the owls: because I give waters in the wilder-*
> *ness, and rivers in the desert, to give drink to*
> *my people, my chosen.*

God's care for His creatures is again the focus in this verse, but there is another element added to the thought. God says the beasts will honor Him. This is not a passive thought. It speaks of an active role for animals.

This verse does not speak of something currently happening, for there is no evidence that animals worship God now. There is no evidence of God consciousness in animals. This truth speaks to something that will be, not something that is.

In the next life, it appears that animals will not only be aware of God, but that they will honor and praise Him just as humans and angels will. This adds a measure of importance to animals in a way not previously imagined. For those who presume animals have no souls or spirits, this truth is very difficult to explain away.

Joel 1:20

The beasts of the field cry also unto thee.

This is another example of passages that lend almost nothing to our study. It does speak of animals and a novice might argue that it speaks of an animal's awareness of God. It does not. When read in context, this verse is clearly addressing God's awareness of animals, specifically their suffering in this present world and not the other way around.

This situation is very similar to when the blood of Abel cried out to God from the ground in Genesis. The blood did not actually cry out, but rather, God was saying that He was aware of the blood and by whom it had been spilled.

Mark 1:12–13

And immediately the spirit driveth him into the
wilderness. And he was there in the wilderness
forty days, tempted of Satan: and was with
the wild beasts; and the angels ministered unto him.

Sometimes it is easy to overlook an important truth in a verse because we are focusing on something larger. In these verses the normal focus would be on the fasting and temptation of Jesus in the wilderness, and rightly so.

However, look at the small string of words that say "and was with the wild beasts." As angels ministered to his needs, the Lord Jesus dwelled among the animals. It doesn't say that he was in the wild where animals lived. It says he *was with* them or companioned by them.

It is apparent that God finds pleasure in the animals that He created. They have a way about them that brings him (and us) pleasure.

Romans 8:18–22

For I reckon that the sufferings of this present time
are not worthy to be compared with the glory which
shall be revealed in us. For the earnest expectation
of the creature waited for the manifestation of the
sons of God. For the creature was made subject to
vanity, not willingly, but by reason of him who hath
subjected the same in hope. Because the creature

itself also shall be delivered from the bondage of
corruption into the glorious liberty of the children of
God. For we know that the whole creation groaneth
and travaileth in pain together until now.

Of all scripture on this topic, I believe these passages are mis-represented the most. I receive much mail from people who read this portion of scripture and jump to the conclusion that it is speaking of animals. I won't deny that there is passive mention of animals, but they are mentioned in context with all of creation.

Truly, the entire creation suffers and travails in pain since man sinned and fell from innocence in the Garden of Eden. Before the fall, everything was perfect. There was no disease, no aging, and no death. All needs were provided for. There was no toil.

That all changed when God's one rule was broken. Man's innocence was lost. The curse of sin was upon our world and all of God's creation has suffered ever since. Imperfection now abounds and all the woes we have today are a result of that fall.

So, in that sense, the whole of creation suffers jointly, including animals. However, in the other verses where the word *creature* is mentioned, it is not talking about animals as many suppose. Verse 20 clearly disqualifies animals as it can only apply to people.

Please remember the rules of exegesis. We must take what is said by the writer (in this case the Apostle Paul) in context. If you read the entire chapter, the topic being discussed has absolutely nothing to do with animals, but addresses rather the conflict of our spirit with our flesh (or carnal mind).

Paul tells us what God's thoughts are on this topic. To imagine that this important dissertation from God would suddenly, without warning, and completely out of context, turn to the topic of animals is just sloppy study.

Verse 1 says, "There is therefore"—and when you see that word "therefore," you must go back to see what it is there for! In verses 15 through 24 of chapter 7, Paul summarizes the ills we have in our weak flesh or "creature." He laments over the wickedness of his own flesh and how he desires to be more spiritual in nature. The flesh or old nature is the focus of chapters 7 and 8 of Romans, and nothing else.

Some will undoubtedly still be hung up on the thought that *creature* can only be used to refer to animals. This is not so, and especially not so in this context. In Colossians 1:15, we have a reference to Jesus being called "the firstborn of every creature."

Surely you will agree that Jesus was not an animal? Obviously, the "creatures" alluded to here are people. Then in verse 23 of that same chapter, we see the gospel was "preached to every creature."

We know that the good news is only for those who need redemption. People need redemption. Animals do not. So, animals do not need the good news preached to them. They are innocent creatures that have no need to be reconciled with God because they were never separated from him as man has been.

There is more . . .

In 2 Corinthians 5:17 it says, "Therefore, if any man be in Christ, he is a new creature."

Galatians 6:15 states, "For in Christ Jesus neither circumcision availeth any thing, nor un-circumcision, but a new creature."

I am sorry to burst the bubble of those relying on these verses to prove that animals have eternal life, but it simply is not saying this. I will concede that verse 22 intimates that the whole of creation suffers and taken in context with everything else offered in this passage, it is clear that animals will have part in the resurrection. Nevertheless, it is a passive thought and not the theme of this portion of scripture.

If mentioning the resurrection in connection with animals sounds outlandish to some, it is not meant to be. I am not trying to be revolutionary or shocking. Through a preponderance of the evidence, we have proved that animals have a place in eternity and that they are not simply left in the dust forever as some erroneously suppose. Given that they are provided for by God and have a place in eternity, we must assume that there is a way for this to occur.

The only way for them to live eternal is through resurrection. I must therefore conclude that they will have a part in it. I don't know how that will work, but that does not concern me. I don't care how God will make it happen. That it will happen is enough for me.

Revelation 5:13

> *And every creature which is in heaven, and on the
> earth, and under the earth, and such as are in the
> sea, and all that are in them, heard I saying,
> Blessing, and honor, and glory, and power, be unto
> him that sitteth upon the throne. And unto the
> Lamb for ever and ever.*

When read in conjunction with Job 12:10, this scripture is very exciting. Here the word *creature* is used differently from the previous passage we looked at. Here it applied collectively of all living things, similar to the use of the word *soul* in Job 12:10.

While the verse addresses the future and eternity of all creatures, we want to focus exclusively on the animals. I have previously discussed this verse in detail, so I will not burden you with discussion here, but I do want to revisit a couple of thoughts and expound upon them.

First, let me ask you, "What more proof do we need?" God, who cannot lie and who does not make mistakes, records that every creature was heard to praise Him. In my mind, *every* is an all-inclusive term meaning *all*. So all creatures is what John (the writer used to pen this book of Revelation) is referring to. Not part, not some, not many, not even most, but all creatures.

By the way, there was no mention of time in this verse. It seems the statement applies to creatures from every period of earth's history. Further, it says "which is in heaven," signifying with quantitative certainty that animals which have passed from this world are currently alive there.

Then, the rest of the verse seems to cover every other conceivable place these creatures could be, whether dead or alive. Again, it says "and *all* that are in them." This leaves no room to question just how many animals this includes. The intent seems clear and unchallengeable to me . . . that again, *all* creatures, angel, animal, or human, are important to God and do not ever cease to exist.

In fairness to opposing views, I took time to approach this verse from every conceivable angle trying to prove that I had arrived at the wrong conclusions and I was unsuccessful. It remains powerful and unshakable evidence to the fact that animals live forever.

John wrote that all creatures would one day worship and praise God. This is the intent of God for His creatures; that they worship and adore Him. Some may not like to hear that. It may not fit into their ideology, or it may be offensive to them, but that does not mitigate the desire of the creator to be worshipped by that which He created. The 148th Psalm is a good starting point if you would like to do your own independent study on this topic.

God's desire is that all of His creation worship and praise Him. As I said earlier, scripture tells us that even inanimate objects like the rocks will praise Him. How is that possible? I have no idea, but I know if God said it, it is so. So, too, when God says "all" will praise Him, I think we should concede that He understood what He was saying and meant it.

God cares about his creation. He loves all the creatures made by His hand. As I said before, the Lord tells us that He clothes the lilies of the field and keeps an eye on the sparrow. He oversees the lives of animals on this earth, directing their seasonal migrations and ensuring that they have adequate sustenance.

His care does not end simply because the physical body gives out. We have already seen that life is not bodies with souls, but rather souls with bodies. He cares about the eternity of the life He has given to all his creatures. God is constant and immutable. He won't care about animals now and not later. That would be a change that was not consistent with His consistency.

I think it is interesting to note that not only does the last book of the Bible (Revelation) make reference to the eternity of animals, but also the first book written, Job (remember, Genesis appears first in the Old Testament, but Job was penned first).

People squabble over the possibility of an animal afterlife, but it appears it was never an issue with God. It was on His mind when He directed the first book to be penned, and remained on His mind when the last book was given.

There are many other passages we could look at that specifically talk about animals and God's providential care for them, but rather than discuss the obvious, I will just let you read a few of them at your leisure. They are:

- 🐾 *Psalm 104*
- 🐾 *Psalm 145: 16, 21*
- 🐾 *Psalm 147:9*

This concludes our study of scripture. I hope you leave this chapter with a new sense of certainty and comfort. The evidence we sought proved to be more than adequate. In fact, it was overwhelmingly convincing. How anyone can argue an opposing view is a mystery to this writer for there is no support for an opposing view.

Chapter 7

ANSWERS TO COMMONLY ASKED QUESTIONS

It is my hope that any questions on your mind concerning animals and God's providence over them were answered satisfactorily in the preceding chapters. Following are responses to specific questions routinely received from pet owners about everyday concerns. I hope these serve to help you deal with any issues you may be battling.

I feel so crushed and so alone. Surely no one has experienced what I am going through. What can I do?

This is one of the most heartbreaking and, unfortunately, one of the most common questions received from people who have lost a pet. For people who love and keep pets, their pet's passing can be one of the most traumatic experiences of their lives. Sometimes the pain can be even greater than when a human friend or loved one passes. I have lost relatives and managed to cope with the loss in a reasonable amount of time, but I have lost pets that I have mourned for years.

There are many and varied reasons why this is so, but I would like to address only the two that seem to be most common to the majority of us. Specifically, they are the special intimacy we enjoy with our pets and their role as perpetual children. Let's discuss these in order.

Our pets are often referred to as our best friends. However, they enjoy a closeness that even our closest human best friends could never expect. This special status allows them to see us at our best, our worst, and everything in between. Without a word being exchanged, our pets know our mood, our intentions, and often what we are thinking.

We are ourselves with our pets as we are with no one else. We let our hair down, so to speak. It may be that we know they cannot tell anyone what they witness, but I suspect that it is more because of the trust we have in their devotion to us. There exists an intimacy that just does not exist in any other relationship.

Even a cherished spouse will make us aware of our faults and try to help us change. Not so our pets. They accept us on an "as is" basis. They don't care if we smoke. They don't care if we have a job. They will snuggle as closely to us when we haven't bathed in a week as they would if we were still wet from the shower. Pets don't ask questions.

They don't point out faults. They just don't care about any of that. Our pets live to be near us. If we had a bad day at the office and come home in a less than cheerful mood, they are there waiting to make us feel better. It doesn't take long for the purring or "thump, thump" of the tail on the floor to make us remember that we are loved, and that is always a cheering thought. We enjoy a closeness and understanding with our pets like we do with nobody else. We are like a brother or sister, friend, confidante, and parents to them all rolled up in one.

This gives me a lead in to the second reason that our pets' passing can be so traumatic for us. We are like parents to them and they perpetual children to us. Children, because they are carefree souls that just love to have a good time. They have no responsibilities to speak of. They just play and sleep their time away. Like children, they depend upon us for everything from learning the rules to sustenance to medical treatment.

Perpetual, because unlike our own children, they never grow up and leave the nest. Animals never marry, never go off to college, and never pursue a career. Consequently, there is never a change in the relationship. There is no relinquishing of responsibility for them.

Everything that happens in their life is usually filtered through us. They don't get outside without our taking or allowing them to go. They don't go off to visit friends. They don't have first dates (or any other for that matter). There is no prom to attend and so forth. Essentially, we not only assume responsibility for our pets, but for their entire life.

Is it any wonder then that when our pets pass away, we suffer more than we do for someone who is not as close as these wonderful personalities and who is not dependent upon us? Not only have we lost a dear family member, but we have lost our closest friend.

If that were not enough, there is also a sense of failure and guilt that as their guardians we could not sustain them and prevent their passing. Subconsciously we blame ourselves for not being able to do more. We play the "what if" game and go over and over again in our minds the circumstances, wondering if we could have done more. It is human nature to have such feelings, but that does not justify them. If you allow those feelings of failure and guilt to prevail, you are going to have a very hard time coping with your loss.

I suggest that instead you take some time to review your life with your best friend. Remember the things you did for him or her. Remember the joy in their lives and how they seemed to spring to life when you were around. Reactions like that come only from feeling loved. Your best friend celebrated your return home each day because he or she knew they were loved and loved you in return.

You made the difference in their life. All living things pass. The best we can hope for is to have been loved in this life. You made their life worth living. You loved your pets and they knew it. Where love prevailed, there is no room for the negative feelings you are beating yourself up with. If you are going to grieve, grieve their absence only. Don't second-guess whether you could have done more for them.

Hold them in your heart, but know that physically they are in another place, a place far superior to the one they left. Suffice it to say that they are alive and well; and know that I would never say anything of such gravity if I were not absolutely sure of my facts.

I had to put my best friend down. I don't know if I did the right thing. Should I have waited longer? Does my pet understand? I feel so guilty, what can I do?

This concern is similar to the one that prompted the question above in that it epitomizes the proverbial "what if" scenario. While every situation is different, my response is always the same. I apply the same response not because I am lazy and do not want to address the individual situation, but rather because I am addressing the guilt and not the factors that lead up to it.

In any event, these questions are hard to answer. If you were to ask me to validate your decision, I could not presumptuously determine that putting your best friend down was the right thing to do. Neither could I suggest that it was the wrong thing to do. I just cannot know.

Similarly, I do not know if the decision was made too soon, too late, or whether it should have been made at all. At best, my thoughts in those areas would be nothing more than a subjective guess based upon very limited information and my own values and level of sensitivity. It would be unfair to hold everyone to my own personal standard and to respond to them based on that alone.

Instead, I encourage you to remember how things were at that moment in time when you bore the responsibility of making that big decision for your family pet. Only you can know if it was the right and timely thing to do. My advice to you is to simply *trust the moment*. By that I mean, that you should not second-guess now, the decision that you made then. Second-guessing will only lead to a feeling of insecurity, which will eventually manifest itself as guilt.

It is imperative to trust that when you were forced to make that undesirable, big decision, you did so from a position of love.

You didn't want to do it. It horrified you to have to decide. Nevertheless, you stepped up and assumed your responsibility. You selflessly decided that your best friend was suffering, that there was nothing you or anyone else could do about it, except make that decision.

Now, long after the fact, divorced from the emotion and pressure of the moment, you are allowing yourself to dissect every thought and circumstance. Now, with the luxury of time, you are starting to re-think the facts and question yourself, playing the "what if" game.

Today, it isn't as clear as it was then. You really don't know if you did the right thing. Take heart, it is human nature to doubt. We are imperfect and fickle creatures. But that does not make it right to pull a load of guilt upon ourselves, and that does not change the reality of the moment when you had to make that big decision.

Don't let your feelings of grief give birth to guilt. Remember the moment. Remember, you wanted nothing more than to help the one you so dearly loved. You would have done anything, paid any amount, performed any feat to prolong their life, but it was just not to be.

The doctor's prognosis was grim. There would be much suffering and pain. The recommendation was to bring them relief, to help them pass on. Under extreme duress and emotional strain, through tears of love, you weighed all the facts, reached down deep inside, put aside your own selfish desire to have your pet hang on, and did what you thought best for them.

At that moment, your love made the selfless decision that rationale and logic now question. There was no selfishness then, but rather a somber consideration of the facts, and a decision to do something that you really did not want to do. But you did it, because someone needed for you to be strong for them.

You put self aside and found strength you did not know you had. Don't let go of that moment. Hold on to it. Trust it. Trust that you were right and that you did what was needed. Trust that your love ruled over your selfishness and know that where your love prevailed, there is no room for guilt or doubt. Grief and sadness are important validations of your love, but do not cheat that process with doubt and guilt. It has no place.

Recently our dog of fifteen years passed away after a long illness. How do I explain to my six-year-old what happened to him?

Losing a precious pet is undoubtedly one of life's most traumatic experiences. It is hard enough for adults to come to grips with their emotions, but when they are responsible for telling their child of a pet's passing, most find it very difficult to do so. How do you deal with such tender hearts? What do you say?

Interestingly, children seem to be more accepting of death than adults. They also appear to heal more quickly. No doubt their innocence is a big factor. Children are too young to have been hardened by life and are more willing to accept explanations that suggest a puppy or kitty heaven. In fact, often they console themselves by making comments like "That's okay . . . I know God will take care of her." Indeed, I have had people tell me that in their attempt to console their child, they wound up being the recipient of comforting words.

Despite this, some adults still seem to have difficulty explaining to children what has become of their pet. Many have solicited me to write a children's version of *Cold Noses at the Pearly Gates*. I have resisted doing so only because I lack the creativity necessary to reach them on their level. I have considered at length how to approach such a project, and always wind up at the same dead end.

However, I do agree that some help needs to be available and so I have done the next best thing. I have developed a letter from an imaginary angel to ease the concerns of a child. Some will balk at this as being just plain stupid and I apologize if it comes across that way to you. The fact is, if you are stressed over how to advise a child about an animal's death, it works.

For what it is worth, here it is.

Dear Megan:

Hello. My name is Helper. I am an angel. There are a lot of angels here in heaven and we all have different jobs. My job is to write to kids and let them know that their pets have arrived in heaven. One of the head angels told me that you were worried about your "Charlie" and asked me to write to you about him.

You will be happy to know that Charlie arrived recently and is doing just swell. I know that he was ill when he was with you. He had gotten very old and when you get old, your body is not as strong as it used to be. Charlie was tired and I think maybe he knew that it was time to come here. And it is a good thing that he did, because now he is not old anymore and he isn't sick either. In fact, I saw him just a little while ago and he was running and jumping with some other dogs and having a great time.

Charlie misses you and hopes that you understand he had to come here. I am sure that one day Charlie will be there to greet you when you come here and you will have a grand reunion. Until then, we will keep him busy and happy. Here we don't have time like you do. It never gets dark. It is just one long day. And everyone here is your friend, so don't worry, Charlie is not ever going to be lonely. Some day when he sees you again, it will be like you had never been apart.

Again, don't feel sad. Charlie is just fine. He is happy and he sends his love to you.

Sincerely,
Helper

Will I ever recover? Will this pain ever lessen or stop?

The short answer is "yes," you will recover and the pain will definitely get better. Eventually it will stop. Offering the short answer, however, does not make the process shorter. There is much that you are going to have to endure. Moments that made you smile when your best friend was here will now as memories bring tears. Pictures, bedding, toys, and even hair balls under the bed will trigger bouts of grief.

Although once a psychology major, I am not a psychologist; but you don't need that credential to have experienced loss and pain. That experience qualifies you to tell others what to expect. Still, these professionals offer tools that can help the grieving heart. So, acquire a good book on grief recovery written by a professional counselor. I do not recommend any one book in particular, for I have found that all generally say the same thing. Just buy one or visit your library and spend some time learning about what you are going through and why.

Depending upon where you are in your loss experience, you are going to go through the stages of shock, denial, deal-making, and anger before you arrive at acceptance's door. And once you cross that threshold, it is hard to say what to expect. Much depends on your own constitution and personality. Some do very well and leave the past behind. If you are like me, you tend to hold on to memories, no matter how painful they can be.

Eventually grief's grip loosens on everyone. Some take weeks. Others like me take years. The process is ever so slow at first, but before you realize it, time, the great healer, has done its work. For a while sights, sounds, even smells will trigger memories, that in turn trigger grief, but with time as your partner, even this will wane.

For some (and definitely not for everyone), a new pet (or another pet already part of the family) will bring relief to their heart. A new personality that devotes itself to you and loves you will give your heart a break from the pain and a way to channel the love you hold and need to express. Many keep themselves from this means of recovery because they feel to get a new pet is to betray the one who has gone ahead. If that is the way you feel, then I recommend you do not cause yourself even more pain by getting a new pet. It would not be fair to either you or the pet.

However, if you can see, as I do, that this is not a betrayal, but rather an act of love that would honor your departed best friend, rescuing one of his or her own kind from a shelter or from an abusive situation, then it might be for you. My heart has a place staked out for each of my buddies who have moved on and that will never change . . . but I have found that pet people have *big* hearts. There is always room for other buddies.

In my case, another pet was necessary to help not only me, but another surviving pet that was having a hard time dealing with the loss. For me, this worked extremely well. It helped me and it helped my other grieving pets. For a short time, it was nothing more than a diversion from the pain, but eventually the new pet brought new joy to our home. This can be a very big step. It is something each of us must weigh carefully. Please think this through well before you acquire another pet. I have seen too many people bring a pet home, only to return it to the shelter because they were not ready. That is so traumatic for an animal.

In any event, time always brings eventual relief from the pain and your life will return to normal. There will be a time when you feel guilty for feeling better, but even that will pass. Nothing will ever take away the sense of absence, but the disabling and relentless grief will subside and eventually disappear. I know it may not seem that way now, but with all the thousands of people I have communicated with over the years, it has proven true every single time.

Everyone says I should get over it—they are tired of my grieving. Why are they so unfeeling? Why can't they understand?

People we respect, people we love, people we trust for support, often do not understand what we are going through when our emotions are impacted by life circumstances. This is especially true if they have never themselves experienced something similar. When we lose a beloved pet, sometimes they say cruel and calloused things, such as "Get over it already, it was just a cat," or "What is your problem, just go buy another dog," simply because they do not understand the depth of our pain.

I want to caution you not to overreact to their lack of understanding. Too many people buy into the philosophy that when you are down and out, you will learn who your true friends are. While this may be true when your house burns down, you get divorced, or you lose your job, I do not think it has any merit when it comes to response (or lack of it) to our grief over the death of a loved one, animal or human.

My strong suggestion is that you not measure your friends by this standard if they do not appear to be there for you when you think they should be. Often, even though it is not obvious, friends and family feel your pain very deeply. They know you are feeling low, but they just do not understand how low and do not know how to react to your grief. They do not know how to approach you or are afraid of saying the wrong thing.

Their first response is usually to try to cheer you up, not realizing that this is the last thing you need or want. That failing, they feel inadequate and unable to help. Perhaps they feel guilty for not being prepared enough to be strong for you, or maybe they feel ashamed that they came across as flippant when they did not mean to. Their own feelings of inadequacy can cause them to be standoffish, but this makes them no less your friend or loved one.

Of course, I am not speaking of those shallow people who say reckless and unkind things to you because they obviously don't care how you feel or because (as unbelievable as this may seem) they have no love for animals whatsoever. It is hard to believe that there are people like that in our world, but we all know someone like that, don't we?

Don't concern yourself with these types of individuals. Do not be angered or offended by their callousness. Somewhere along the way, they missed out on learning compassion, possibly because they were never shown any themselves. Their comments should be assigned "zero gravity" so that they sort of just float away. Cast them off and forget them. They have already suffered great loss in this life by not having known the devotion and love of a precious pet.

For those people who obviously care, but who cannot find a way to show it, or are afraid of dragging you down even further, try to understand and accept what they are going through. In all probability your pain is of great importance and concern to them, but they just do not know what to do to help.

If you want to avoid the frustration and added pain of someone you care about acting this way, be proactive. If it appears they do not understand your pain or that they are uncomfortable, try to educate them and set them at ease. I have found that saying something to them first often helps. For example:

I know what I am going through is difficult for you to understand. I know you would help me if you could, but there is really nothing you can do right

now. I need to go through this. If you would just
give me some time and be patient, eventually my
pain will be manageable and I will start being my
old self again.

Then, you need to follow through on your promise. Grieve as long as you must, but start to focus on positive things as soon as you are able to. Know that your best friend is not suffering and that this pet is in a far better place than we could ever imagine. Know, too, that you are not to blame, no matter what the circumstances. Things happen. Sometimes they are bad things. You are the type of individual who would do anything to help your pet. If it was in your power, if you could have done something, anything . . . you would have! There is no room for guilt in unconditional love like that. Time and focus will help you become the person you were and you will see that friends and family are still there for you.

Forgive friends and family their inability to relate to what you are going through. It doesn't mean they don't care. It doesn't mean they do not love you. In fact, in most cases you will find that it is because they care, because they love you, that they either say or do stupid things or keep their distance because they don't know what to do.

Grieving is one of the few times when we are allowed to be selfish and to overindulge if we want to. You take your time in this very private matter. Set those who care about you at ease and let them know you require time to grieve and be alone. Then grieve as long as you need to. But when you are finished, return to normal for them. The pain will still be there, but you will have framed it in context with the rest of your life and will still have friends and loved ones by your side.

I know this is a difficult thing to ask of someone who is in the throws of grief, but if the people in your life are important to you, you must take the initiative to ensure your relationships do not suffer.

Do animals have souls? My pastor told me that animals do not have souls. I am so upset. How can this be?

I have addressed this question in other chapters of this book at least twice. Understanding that some people "skim" read, I am going to repeat it here one more time in hopes that doing so will help someone.

It is true that there are a number of my fellow ministers who take this view, but rest assured their position is both erroneous and unsupportable. In fact, I find this view to be both presumptuous and theologically immature. Presumptuous, because the Bible is clear that God valued the creatures he formed with his own hands and called them "very good," indicating that their existence pleased him. The Bible gives record that God, motivated by this pleasure and His love, personally and purposely protects and provides for His creatures from Eden past through millennium future.

Indeed, his original plan in Eden was that animals (like humans) would live forever. His immutability precludes variance from that plan, irrespective of the temporary setback caused by the fall of mankind. It is presumptuous to think that God would change His mind on this matter, for His thoughts and plans are perfect and never in need of correction or change.

Moreover, I find the idea that animals have no souls theologically immature and lacking. The evidence found in scripture does not support such a position, quite the opposite. It seems many ministers are content to accept (and pass on to others) what they heard from their seminary professor rather than study the topic for themselves. This reflects spiritual laziness and a lack of concern for the feelings of their congregants.

I do not mean to reflect negatively on seminary professors or anyone else, but when you rely solely on the ideas of someone else without ensuring scripture supports those ideas, you are asking for trouble. God warns us to "search out a thing whether it be true" and to "study to show thyself approved." A shortcut around God's method of "knowing a thing" will often lead one to an erroneous view.

Such is the case with animals and the question of whether they are eternal or temporal creatures. Let us follow God's advice and see what His word has to say on the topic. Following is only a glimpse of the overall picture, but it will serve our purpose. Job 12:10 says, *"In whose hand is the soul of every living thing."*

The word *soul* is used in over twenty different ways in the Bible. Invariably, when people come across this word in scripture, they automatically associate it with redemption, so much so that no matter in what context it is used, the connection to salvation is always present in their minds and applied to the interpretation. In most cases, this is right and acceptable, but there are times when it is not.

Clearly, the gospel message is not for animals. It is exclusively for people. It is a reconciliatory outreach from God to those in need of salvation, or sinners. However, to allow this truth to cause one to draw the conclusion that animals therefore cannot have souls is to visit a gross injustice on scripture. In fact, the Hebrew word *nephesh* (soul), appears many times in scripture and is used interchangeably to describe both the essence of man and animals. It does not make a distinction between the two and it does not delve into the doctrine of salvation.

This passage in Job is a good example of this point. The word soul is not used in relation to redemption, but rather addresses providential care. A better rendering of its meaning in this verse would be "the life or essence of every living thing." God is speaking of that part of people and animals that contains or houses the "life" he has given to them.

When we mesh this thought in Job with Romans chapter 8 and Revelation 5:9–13, the meaning is clear, the life or essence of every living thing is in the hand of God and every living thing is made eternal, not temporal.

However, this word in Job indicates an even deeper thought for us to consider. We often refer to man as a flesh-and-blood body with a soul, but in truth, in keeping with the absolute intent of this word nephesh, man is a soul that has been placed in a flesh-and-blood body. The distinction is subtle, but it is immense in effect. This is our essence, that we are a soul, not a body. The body is temporal, but the soul eternal.

This truth applies to animals as well for the same word (nephesh) is used . . . they are not creatures with souls, but are eternal souls (or essences) given temporary bodies. The difference is, unlike humans, and much like the angels, animals need no redemption. So when we refer to their souls, we are merely acknowledging that they have essence and that this essence is eternal in nature, not that they need redemption like humans. They are innocent creatures whose souls are safe in the hand of their creator. The overwhelming evidence is that the soul of an animal is as eternal as the soul of man.

Why does my dog eat grass?

I think we would be hard pressed to find anyone who has not witnessed this peculiarity of domestic animals at one time or another. When it is our pet, however, it causes us concern and, if we let our imaginations go unchecked, it can cause us alarm.

It has been my experience that on occasion, that alarm can lead to unnecessary expense as we panic and rush our best friend off to the nearest veterinarian, only to hear him tell us with a chuckle "He's okay, it's normal for him to eat grass." How embarrassing is that!

Why is it normal for our pets to consume grass? They all do it if they are allowed access to it. Are they not getting the right nourishment? Are they ill? These are all unsettling, but reasonable questions.

More unsettling is that invariably shortly after ingesting the grass, perhaps twenty minutes later, they regurgitate it back up in a kind of green gooey mess (sorry to be so graphic). Why would they do this? Why would they do something that appears to be so hard on their system, or maybe even harmful to them? Should I be alarmed?

The short answer is "No, don't panic." As I mentioned earlier, any veterinarian will tell you that this is normal behavior. The very fact that all pets do it should suggest to you that it is not a bad thing.

The long or more detailed answer is that the outdoors is an animal's natural world and grass is part of that world. You and I can turn on the radio or television and be kept up to date on what is happening in our world. For dogs and cats, the ground is their primary source of connection with their world.

The ground is like a giant newspaper for them. They interpret the odors and conditions to discover what other dogs have been visiting their turf and what they did there. They "read" the yard to know what is happening in the world outside the house. With their heightened senses, they perceive when another dog or cat has been on their turf, whether it rained the night before, that so-and-so is in heat, or that the season is changing.

Additionally, the role the ground plays in our pets' lives does not end at bringing them the news. Through their own "contributions," they communicate to future visitors of that site who the yard belongs to, who they are, and what they are about. Sometimes the deposit is meant as a welcome, other times a warning. It just depends on what the news is for that day.

But in keeping with the primary theme of my answer, the ground is also the local canine and feline drug store. Perhaps it could more accurately be called the local natural herb store.

I don't know how many times I have heard someone ignorantly say, "Look at that stupid dog eating grass." The truth is, dogs are not stupid at all, but are rather quite savvy natural pharmacists. I think most people would be surprised to learn that animals know a whole lot more about herbs than we do. I concede it may be more of an instinctive knowledge than cognitive understanding, but it is knowledge nonetheless.

In fact, animals' understanding of herbal remedies is awesome.

Have you ever noticed that they don't eat just any grass . . . they sniff around until they find exactly what they are looking for? Like the aisles in a drug store, each section of the outdoors holds different remedies.

For instance, certain grasses and sprouts are sought out and taken as internal cleansers. They cause vomiting; something we have all witnessed. This vomiting is the expected result for your pet. They know when they eat it that it will cause this reaction, yet they do it willingly and with purpose.

They instinctively know that it will cleanse their body of bile and other items that are not digestible. Anyone who loves and keeps animals knows that there are many items that qualify in this category, from shoes to yarn to hair to some of the most extraordinary items.

While it is unsettling to know that they are not smart enough to figure out that swallowing a sock is not a good thing, it is comforting that pets are usually savvy enough to know how to extricate it from their system before it becomes a problem or threat. This only emphasizes the importance of their having access to the outdoors on a regular basis.

In addition, there is more to their natural pharmacy than just cleansers. Other grasses and herbs help evict or terminate worms and other parasites in their system. Still others provide needed minerals and nutrients and enhance digestive enzymes and acids. Uncannily, animals seem to know what remedy is needed for exactly whatever ails them at the moment.

Then, perhaps the biggest benefit to them is the presence of chlorophyll in most grasses. Chlorophyll helps to fight infection, enrich the coat, and even relieves pain such as joint aches. It can also enhance cartilage soundness and offers a host of other benefits.

I know all this sounds a bit simplistic, but it really is not that complicated. The truth is that animals appear to know more about these things than you and I do and certainly more than we would think they should know. I am not sure "how" they know, but it is enough to accept that they do know, without having to know the "why."

Modern medicine has actually taken a step backward to develop more primitive remedies as a result of a closer study of this savvy in animals. Science now recognizes that many of the grassroots (pardon the pun) remedies nature provides for our pets are as good as, if not better than, synthetic drugs.

In fact, people are learning how to cultivate and produce certain herbs and grasses to help their pets, even freezing summer crops for winter dispensing when grasses are not in season. This can be especially helpful to cats and other mammals who are not allowed to venture outdoors, but who still need to ingest some of the natural cleansing agents found there.

Next time you see your pet eating grass, don't worry it. They are doing something to help their health. Just give them time to allow the process to culminate before you let them back in on your carpet.

My dog is a really good dog, but she sometimes snaps at strangers when we are at the park? What can I do about this?
The Humane Society has gone on record stating that dog bites

have become an epidemic. While I agree that the more than 5 million annually recorded bites are of epidemic proportions, it is nonsense to categorize dog bites themselves as an epidemic. They are not a contagious disease that has been allowed to continue unchecked and there is no connection between the bite of one dog and another.

Furthermore, I reject the premise that dog bites are always a deliberate action on the part of dogs. Rather, most dog bites are a reaction to some external stimulus. I am not suggesting that biting is a justifiable reaction, only that the reaction is often explainable. There are reasons that dogs become aggressive and violent.

I will concede that sometimes dogs attack without any apparent provocation, but somehow the public gets the message that all dog bites are of this variety. It seems the media's thirst for the sensational has caused them to focus more on extreme examples of bad dog behavior rather than presenting the whole story.

A more balanced representation of both unprovoked and provoked attacks by the media would be much fairer to this noble animal. Additionally, such an approach might help educate the public on how to avoid being bitten by a dog rather than cause them to panic every time they see an unleashed canine.

Sadly, the result of one-sided press is usually lower public tolerance and ultimately, unspeakable carnage for a species of animal whose history has been one of service and companionship to us. For each dog bite there are a million wagging tails and sloppy kisses that go unreported. Yet each day in our country many dogs are put down simply because they exhibited aggressive behavior.

I am not saying that we should give these animals a free pass. I am saying rather that with a little more awareness and effort, most dogs can be trained to be non-aggressive and the public can be made aware of how to avoid being bitten.

If you keep a dog, there are certain things you need to do to ensure that your animal does not develop aggressive behavior. He or she may display good behavior in your presence, but you want to make sure they act the same way when you are not around. There are certain steps each responsible dog owner should take to help their best friend develop properly. Here is an acronym to help you remember several critical points in ensuring that your dog is a "good boy/girl." The word is STOP (as in "stop them from biting").

> **S**—*Spay or neuter.* Only about 25 percent of dog bites come from dogs that have been spayed or neutered. There are differing opinions as to why, but whatever the reason, it works. Aside from the other advantages of having this procedure performed, give your best friend a head start on developing good behavior by having them spayed or neutered.

> **T**—*Training.* Formal, professional training is best, but if you would rather do the job yourself, consult with experts or read leading books on the topic. Make sure your dog responds not only to your commands, but to those of your immediate family. Train them to be sociable with those of your household and with visitors. Do not isolate them in the

backyard on a chain. This almost guarantees behavioral problems. Rather, expose them to people in positive situations and teach them to be comfortable around them.

O—*Observation.* If possible, observe how your dog acts around other people without them knowing you are watching. Also, consider setting up a video camera in the home while you are gone for a few hours to see how they react to outside noise, telephone rings, deliveries, other pets, and so on. This may seem an extreme measure, but you may be surprised at what you find. If you discover problems, go back to "T" above to correct them.

P—*Play.* Playing is important to an animal, just as it is to people. As silly as this may sound, they need a diversion from their life of leisure, a time to get excited and to burn up energy. Play games with them. Run through the woods with them. Go swimming with them. Avoid anything that would promote aggressive behavior like saying "sic 'em" when you see a bird or squirrel, but make them use up their energy in positive ways.

Balls were made for children and dogs. Use them. Make them have a good time and they will be happy. The worst thing I ever saw a happy dog do was slobber all over someone. That may make them manners challenged, but it does not make them a bad dog. Make sure that your pet knows the difference between being good and being bad. If they are properly trained and socialized, they should be able to understand the difference.

Now then, this takes care of your dog, but what about the dogs of others? What can you do to protect yourself and your family from a dog that has not been trained and socialized properly when they display aggressive and threatening behavior? Let's employ another acronym. The word this time is SCARS (as in how to avoid getting them from an aggressive dog).

S—*Strangers.* You should be very cautious when you approach or are approached by a strange dog. Of course, the danger is relative depending on the size of the dog. I don't think an angry Chihuahua is as much a threat to someone as an annoyed Doberman, for example; so exercise appropriate caution. Remember that the dog doesn't know you either and to them, you are large and threatening in your own right. You make them feel uncomfortable.

C—*Control.* When you are in a situation where a strange dog is displaying aggressive behavior toward you, try to control the way you react. The old axiom that animals can smell fear probably is better stated that they can "see" fear. If a dog growls at you and you react by taking off screaming and running like a Saturday-morning cartoon character, the dog is probably going to chase you.

Each situation is different, but generally speaking, it is a good idea not to turn and run, not to scream, and not to make eye contact with the animal. If the dog approaches you, keep your arms, legs, and hands close to your body. Maintaining control is important. It is akin to not splashing in the water when a shark is around. You don't want to draw attention to yourself.

A—*Awareness.* Don't surprise a sleeping dog. Make them aware that you are there. They can be startled just like people, and their initial reaction is going to either be that they run off with their tail between their legs, or that they stand and defend themselves. The former is preferred over the latter, but there is no guarantee this is how they will react when disturbed.

Therefore, when approaching a sleeping dog, or one that is otherwise preoccupied and does not see your approach, make it a point to make them aware of your presence long before you are close enough to startle them. Often they will just give an initial cursory bark and then go about their business.

R—*Respect.* If at all possible, adherence to the old cliché "let sleeping dogs lay" is a good rule to follow. Some dogs wake up as grumpy as people do and it is better to just let them sleep. Additionally, dogs that are eating, feeling ill, pregnant, or nursing a litter require a little more respect than the dog that comes up to you wagging their tail. Just as we covet our personal space, they want theirs, too. Respect their needs and you will have fewer problems.

S—*Substitute.* If all else fails and you are certain that an attack is imminent, be ready to substitute an article of clothing or something you are carrying in place of your body. We have all seen the nature documentary where a hiker throws his backpack to a charging bear. The bear stops to investigate this "present," affording the hiker valuable time to make his escape. Dogs are curious creatures, too. If you throw your purse or shirt or shoe in its path, the chances are good that the animal will stop to investigate. You can always come back later and get your belongings.

In summation, most dog attacks do not have to happen. They can be avoided. It only takes a little effort on the part of dog owners and common sense on the part of the rest of us.

Chapter 8

SOME FINAL THOUGHTS

I hope this book has proven to be a tremendous help to you. As I pointed out earlier, my goal was singular . . . to give comfort to those in need. I wanted that help to provide emotional benefit to you, but it was necessarily also spiritual in nature. I wanted to reach beyond any help this old world could offer and give readers the comfort that their animals are alive and well, and also a hope of seeing them again.

I don't care about sales or gaining fame. For me, being a successful author is secondary to being a helpful Christian. My desire is to help others by providing trustworthy answers to the questions that accompany loss of a pet. To that end, I want to emphasize one final time that this book is not speculative, except in those areas where I was careful to point out that I was expressing opinion rather than fact. And even then, I based my opinion upon some very solid principles.

My training in Bible doctrine, apologetics, and rules of exegesis has been mentioned sufficiently to validate that my research and conclusions were not flippant, but well thought out. Additionally, I think my candid and open approach reflects my honesty, and hopefully my integrity as well. I would rather perish than misrepresent the Word of God.

There is no doubt but that animals are eternal creatures, like all the other creatures God made. To think otherwise is to take an unsupportable and baseless position that is contrary to His word. Moreover, to hold that animals will simply cease to exist or be annihilated both minimizes the worth of these wonderful personalities and makes God out to be a villain.

It is simply preposterous to say that God, who created them and gave them life, including personalities, emotions, and the ability to reason, did so only to destroy them in the end. This would mean that He not only made a mistake in creating them, but that He does indeed change his mind, which in turn makes Him as flawed as you or I. And if that were true, than what keeps Him from changing His mind about you and me?

If we place our trust in Him and He suddenly and whimsically changed His mind about His love for us based upon how we lived, where would that leave us? I assure you, considering my own inconsistent Christian deportment, I would be in a very leaky boat. Thank God He is not like me, but He is constant and immutable. Thank God we can depend on Him and do not have to depend on ourselves.

God has not changed His mind about the animals. He has made provision for them. In truth, they really are His animals, and not ours. They belong to the one who created them and gave them life. They are merely on loan to us, and as inconceivable as it may seem, God loves them more than you and I ever could.

You and I would do anything to provide for our best friends.

If we could extend their lives by just a day, we would spare no expense. Alas, we have no power over life or death. God also would do anything to provide for his animals. In fact, He does. Unlike us, God does have power and authority over life and death. He not only feeds, clothes, and provides for animals in this life in ways we are not even aware of, but when our pets pass and we are helpless to do anything but grieve, God ushers them into eternity, safe in his care.

I believe that with all my heart. I would never say anything with this much gravity if I were not absolutely certain of what I was claiming. I have never said anything just because I thought it was what someone wanted to hear. People need to hear the truth. They want to hear the truth. In this case, the truth just happens to be the thing we want to hear.

I have almost concluded my thoughts and presentation on the topic of animal afterlife. I hope that what has been said thus far has helped you. I said in the beginning that you might start this book a skeptic. If you did, I hope that what I have given you has provoked you to a new understanding of what life is and how very important it is to the one who gives it to his creatures. This was a very key objective for me. Like the famed Billy Sunday, my ministry springs from Isaiah 61:1, in particular that portion that admonishes me to "bind the brokenhearted."

As important as that goal is, there is an even more important point that I am compelled to discuss, one that I have put off until now. My service to you will be incomplete if I do not take the time to address it here. Yet, I hesitate, because I know what I have to say may not sit well with some. I hope you will understand that I have no choice in this matter.

As I said above, I am compelled to speak of this. I am acutely aware that some will accuse me of preaching, but my intent is not to preach, but to fulfill my promise and complete my task of bringing you hope. The truth is a funny thing. If you give only half the story, it really is not the truth, but rather a lie. I will not lie. Accordingly, to use the term a very great American has coined, I want to give you the "rest of the story."

And the rest of the story is this . . . I can assure you that our beloved best friends are safe and well in the presence of their creator. They no longer suffer. They no longer are subject to the ills they endured in this world. If there was brief pain associated with their passing, that pain is not even a memory for them now. It, along with the rudimentary shortcomings of this world, is far removed from their new life. This I know without doubt, by faith in the solid evidence offered by the Bible.

I am absolutely sure of this when it comes to these wonderful creatures God made and loves. I can, in a sense, speak for them, and report that they live. However, I cannot make the same claim for people, and that is the rest of the truth I am compelled to give you.

As I said at the beginning of this book, animals do not need faith, because they do not need reconciliation. According to the same Bible we used to establish this truth, it says people are not so. People do need faith and reconciliation. It is between them and God and I have no authority, nor have I the ability to know who has placed faith in God or not.

If I could pass along my faith to you, I would do so without hesitation. Unfortunately, faith comes from within, not without. Faith is something generated by the individual. The best I can do is to try to explain faith from a Bible perspective for you without being offensive. Without a personal faith in the Lord, we are told that we have no place in His presence. Since I do not know if you have met with the Lord on his terms, I cannot assure you about your own spiritual condition. I have neither the authority nor the right to do so.

Jesus said, "I am the way, the truth and the life, no man (or woman) cometh unto the father but by me" (John 14:6). The measure then is that God's reconciliation depends on your coming to Him through the work that the Son did. I read that verse over and over again and nowhere does it mention me as the one who decides your spiritual condition. It is between you and God and no one else.

If you are angry with me for having said all that, consider this. I never mentioned your name. I do not even know you. If you are upset with the verse I just quoted, maybe you should consider who wrote it. I assure you these are not my words. I merely quoted from a far superior book. I suggest you take your concerns to its author.

I realize some will still say I was too strong or too preachy in what I said above. I cannot help that. I carefully selected my words to be both kind and provoking. What kind of a person would I be, if knowing the whole truth, I only told you the half? There is too much of that in the world already and I want no part of it.

Please believe me when I say that I had no ulterior motive in making this final case. It was for your good and your good only that I presented it at all. I gain nothing by exposing myself to the ire and ridicule of those who disagree with the Bible. I provide the PETGATE e-mail address for those who have additional questions or have a need to talk with someone who understands, but some have chosen to use it to admonish me for caring about their spiritual condition.

Moving on to a completely different topic, I purposely avoided issues involving the psychological recovery process of grief. Although I have a lot of experience counseling grieving people, I am not legally qualified to do so. Moreover, even if my credentials were recognized and accepted by appropriate authorities, there would be no need for me to exercise them. There already exists an abundance of excellent literature on the subject, and an army of professionals to assist you. I could add nothing new.

Ideally, it would be best if we never suffered pet loss. Unfortunately, on this earth, the only way that you could accomplish this would be to refrain from having pets altogether. For me, and I imagine many others like me, this would be a fate worse than enduring a loss.

People like me have no alternative. We are pet and animal lovers. Our lives would be empty without their wonderful personalities and love. They are the most unassuming, uninhibited creatures God ever made. They don't care if you are in a bad mood or if you didn't have time to shower. They just want to be near you, to purr in your lap, to fill your room with their chirping, to bang a dent in the wall with their happy tail.

The people in your life all have played different roles, each important in its own way and right. Each of them influenced and impacted your life in different ways. If any of them had not played their part, you may not have realized that something was missing, but it would have been missing nonetheless.

The same holds true with our pets. They play an extremely

important role in our life. So even though abstinence from keeping a pet may seem like a sure way to not suffer loss, in fact, you would have suffered loss already. For those of us who are hooked, there is no alternative anyway.

Given that we understand that keeping pets eventually leads to the misfortune of losing them, there are some precautions we can take to ensure their best possible longevity and quality of life. It begins with selecting our pet. Whether it be a kitten, puppy, parakeet, rabbit, hamster, or whatever, we want to select an animal that appears to be healthy.

Now, I know there are some people who purposely seek out sick and dying animals to make a loving home for them before they pass. I do not mean to belittle your efforts or cause anyone so inclined to reconsider. We need people like you. Rather, our animal friends need people like you. You are their heroes and heroines. My gratitude is extended to you on behalf of all those who cannot thank you.

My suggestions here are meant for those who do not know much about animals or for those who are not prepared to deal with an animal that is ill or potentially ill from the start. These folks need to be careful. Acquiring an animal that has overwhelming needs that you cannot meet will usually mean that animal will suffer more and not get the care it needs from someone else who is more prepared and able to deal with the medical issue. Please avoid that situation. Consider the animal's needs first before you make a decision.

Be careful of quick attachments as well. I know those big brown eyes can just grab you and make your mind up for you. Once you are smitten, you are smitten. It doesn't matter if the animal is missing a leg or has green fur . . . if you have fallen for it, you have fallen. So exercise caution. There is no known remedy for "smittenitis." I give this advice out as a hypocrite, for I have suffered from the disease myself. In fact, my case is chronic.

If, however, you are not overwhelmed by the purring or snuggling or wrinkly little nose and you can maintain some semblance of composure and restraint, it would do you well to check the animal over as thoroughly as possible. I admit that this takes a fair amount of detachment and coolness, which can lead to guilt. I even feel a bit guilty writing these words, but the goal here is to give the animal the best home and the best chance. Accordingly, if you cannot handle the ailments and associated medical expenses, or if you are not prepared for the possible early loss of that animal to its ailment, I suggest you take the time to look over and choose your pet carefully.

Here are some questions you might ask yourself before making up your mind. This is not a complete list, nor is it scientific. You may want to add to the list depending on what you want the animal for (e.g., breeding, shows, mascot). So tailor your checklist to your personal needs as well as the needs of the animal.

1. Is there any obvious discolored or missing fur, feathers?
2. Lift the tail. Are hookworms present or signs of diarrhea?
3. Does the stomach area seem bloated? (indicating worms)
4. Does the animal appear lethargic or weak?
5. Is the animal's voice raspy or hoarse when they bark, etc.?
6. Is the animal able to follow hand movement without problem?

7. Are there any visible defects (e.g., limping, missing hair)?
8. Does the animal appear to have equilibrium problems?

This is not a complete list by any means, but if any of these problems are apparent, chances are you will have to make some big decisions. There are a lot of other things you could look for depending upon the type of pet you are seeking. I restricted my comments and checklist to small mammals and birds, but these same principles may be applied easily to just about any creature. If you are unfamiliar with the animal, obtain literature and read, read, read, before you make a decision. The more you know the better for you and the animal.

Once you have completed your tailor-made checklist and satisfied yourself that the animal you are considering is a good fit for your lifestyle, consider enlisting the help of a professional to give a more quantitative medical evaluation. However you acquire your pet, whether a gift or purchase, or if it just shows up on your doorstep, you should take the animal for a checkup to a veterinarian. I don't want to sound like your mother (or mine), but better safe than sorry. Often, if you catch an ailment early, its negative effects can be held to a minimum.

A quick look-see by the doctor or other professionals will usually cost between $25 and $40, but it could save you thousands, and a lot of anxiety and grief. For that minimal cost a professional will perform a sort of mini-physical examination. Essentially, they will give it a quick visual once-over (yes, I know you already did that), look into the eyes, ears, nose, mouth and the other, southern, end as well.

The doctor will nod and "umm-hmmm" and usually tell you

that everything looks fine. In those instances where they are not as confident that everything looks fine, they may suggest blood work or other tests. But again, it is better to catch any potential ailment early.

It may be a good practice to enter at least a verbal agreement with the breeder or pet store owner that you are going to have the animal checked by a veterinarian and if something serious is discovered, they agree to pay for the remedy. Or, if they are unwilling to do this, that they agree to take the animal back and refund your money. Speaking strictly from a business perspective, that is only fair. You are not asking them to pay for the medical examination, and you are not asking them to guarantee the animal for life. You just want to make sure they are selling you a healthy pet.

Then, in those rare cases where something serious is discovered and greater expense is certain, you can ask the seller to foot the bill, or, that failing, ask them to refund your money. Now, in the final analysis, the seller may not honor the verbal agreement. If this happens, you will have to weigh your moral and legal options and do as your heart dictates.

If it were me, I would simply absorb the cost myself. In fact, let me completely expose my hypocrisy by telling you that each of my three current animals had some sort of defect when I acquired them. It didn't matter. I was hooked in minutes. How can anyone look in those loving and lonely eyes and deny them. They seem to say, "Here I am, here I am, take me, take me—I don't like this place, let me come to your house."

So I am a hypocrite. I am quick to give sound advice, but I come up short when it comes to taking it. Each of my buddies were medically defective and unwanted by anyone else. They lacked the luster that perhaps medically sound animals possess, but I took them and all the responsibilities that went with them anyway. And as I think of the joy we have brought each other, I don't think it much matters.

Returning to my thoughts concerning an initial medical examination . . . most states require (and common sense dictates) that your animals receive certain vaccinations each year. Since you already have to pay for the office visit, what is a few dollars more to check for parasitical invaders or abnormalities?

Don't be a cheapskate when it comes to your pet. Just because your dog remains in a fenced yard and never wanders into the woods or city, don't think disease cannot reach them. I have had so many letters from people who felt their animal was safe in their little townhouse yard. They decided not to get a parvo vaccination. They saved a few dollars, but would have probably paid 100 times that to have their best friend back.

There is a lot of responsibility associated with a pet. Canines and felines need vaccinations. Not just rabies, but parvo, distemper, kennel fever, and sometimes more. Birds need clipping and exact diets. I could list a variety of animals and their needs if I had both room and time. Suffice it to say, the expense of maintaining a healthy pet is sometimes significant. The dividends are usually a longer, healthier life. Conversely, a lack of proper medical regimen can spell a shorter, unhealthy life. If you cannot afford to take care of an animal, you should never take it home.

Another important consideration impacting upon health and longevity is diet. A good diet is essential to growth, appearance, health, and long life. I feel like such a fool addressing this topic for I am the biggest offender of ensuring a good diet for my pets.

I know that good nutrition, correct portions, and little junk food are paramount to good health in our pets, but I am a pushover. They have my number. . . . I am an easy mark and they know it. My wife can sit and eat a meal and tune out the begging dog. Funny thing, but it is interesting to note that the begging dog tunes her out, too. They know she is not going to budge. So, they turn their attention to me, the "mark." And I crumble and start handing out my meal. To quote comedian Lou Costello, an old friend from my hometown who is no longer with us, "I am a baaaaaad boy."

Cats are just as bad, or worse. I cannot have cats any longer since my wife developed an allergy to their fur, but most of us know that when it comes to being finicky, cats have it all over dogs. If you don't give them what they want, not only will they turn their noses up, but when you are not looking, they will hunt down and help themselves to something more to their liking.

Please do not indict me for ruining my dog's diet. My intentions are the best. I purchase any number of solid, scientific diet plans. I spare no cost. It's the dogs' fault. They won't eat it. I buy it, I put it in their bowl, I tell them it is good for them. I even pretend to eat it myself and add a very convincing "ummm" to the presentation. But they just won't eat it.

Fortunately, my saving grace here is that very probably you are as guilty as I am in this matter. You are, aren't you? Sure you are. You know you are.

How about if we determine together that we are going to put our pets on a healthier diet? Let's agree that we are going to be strong and resolute and not give in to the merciless tactics of our pets that deprive us of our dinners.

Finally, we need to exercise our animals. That may be difficult if you keep birds or fish, but if you give those types of pets enough room, they will exercise themselves. Cats usually stay in fairly good shape on their own, but I have seen some that appeared to be runaway balloons from a parade. Dogs are much easier to exercise because most of them love to play and run. They will chase just about anything you throw for them until they tire of doing so. I have also found that if you give a dog a swimming pool or a small pond, there is no end to the exercise they will get.

I regularly exercise my dogs and it shows in their appearance and in their general good health. Perhaps that is why I don't feel so very guilty about the junk food I sometimes give to them. They just do not sit around all day doing nothing. They have access to the backyard anytime they want to go—and they chase up and down the fence after squirrels, rabbits, leaves, and sometimes absolutely nothing.

What's more, the more they exercise, the more they want to exercise. My Westie and I play "fetch the ball" daily. I throw it and she fetches it some thirty-five times or more. I put the ball aside thinking we are done and she seems to agree with me, to a point. She thinks Yes, we are done fetching. . . . *the ball* . . . but we have so many other toys here to fetch.

So then she brings me her chew toy, and then the pull socks, and then this and that, until finally we have gone through her entire inventory of toys. Finally, she tires of fetching altogether and lays down. I start toward my easy chair and she quickly jumps up and play-growls "arrraff," which means "Not so fast—we haven't played the pull game yet." And so she goes through the entire inventory again and presents me with each article.

If I sound as if I am complaining, I am not. I actually enjoy spending time with my dogs and expending energy along with them. It keeps us both in shape and enhances their quality and quantity of life. If you keep pets, don't confine them to a small cage or tie them to a tree all day, every day. Get outside with them and play and run and enjoy each other. Give them something exciting to look forward to each day.

Make every day count. Love them and treat them well while they are with you. They aren't with us nearly long enough. Don't ever trap yourself into wasting time you could spend with them now and regretting it later. We will see them again, but that might be a very long time.

Stories of Humor

I sincerely hope this book has found its mark in your heart and manifested itself in the form of hope and encouragement. If it has, you are now equipped with the wherewithal to handle the pain and emptiness that you once could not cope with. The uncertainty has been replaced with an understanding that you will one day see again that wonderful animal who so filled your life. The dark cloud that hung over you now has a very pronounced silver lining. There is still pain and longing because of your pet's absence, but that is now manageable. Now the longing is fueled by hope and not grief.

I want the final pages to close our time together on a very positive note. I want to share a few more stories with you here. In the body of the book I used stories to help illustrate or emphasize a point. Here they are offered for no other reason but to provide a diversion for your mind and some levity to your heart.

I think when we share our stories with each other, it helps. It lets us know that we are not alone, that God or life or fate has not singled us out to suffer and no one else. This in turn helps us to put our situation in proper perspective. Many of you have shared your stories with me and we have wept together. Now, I want to share some of the memories I have of my departed pets so that you will know that this writer can relate to your pain. I miss each of them as much today as I did thirty years ago. They are absent in my present life, but remain present in my heart.

Don't worry. None of the stories will add to your sadness. Some are humorous; some are inspiring; and all are uplifting. I have not embellished upon them in the slightest. I hope they make you smile and warm your heart.

Then, I will provide some daily helps that you might find useful.

Let's begin with a story from my childhood best friend, Scooter, and then just move ahead in no particular order.

Scooter and the "Kitty"

The first dog I ever had was a wonderful animal that cost me all of my twelfth-year birthday money. Scooter came out of a cardboard box sitting in a department store, marked $4.99. He was perhaps the best bargain of my young life. He was definitely the best investment, for he paid out years of devotion and friendship that my human friends could never give me. He was a great dog, protective and faithful. He never wandered more than twenty feet from me when I and my friends went out playing in the fields that bordered the local river or railroad tracks.

On one of our escapades, Scooter and I were at one of our favorite places, a place that probably accounts for many of the gray hairs on my mother's head. We were in the woods, across the railroad tracks from our clubhouse where industrial marble slabs were stored. The marble slabs were huge, as wide as the widest refrigerator and twice as long, weighing several tons. The slabs were stacked four or five high with railroad ties between the slabs to give the stacks stability.

Scooter

There were easily hundreds of stacks in about a two-acre parcel of land. Each stack was different in shape and stability. Some, we learned, would wobble when you jumped on them from another stack, much like the trick stones on some Disney rides.

My club, which consisted of six or seven preteen boys and our dogs, used this marble yard to hide and play in, to blow off fireworks, or to climb the stacks to reach the ripest mulberries on the big trees. It was a grand place that we all loved with the same passion our mothers loathed it. Many a nearly fractured skull had come crying home from this enchanting place.

On this occasion, only Scooter and I were in the marble yard. I was jumping from stack to stack above, while he chased me from twenty feet below. The fact that I could have fallen and split my head open (again) did nothing to keep us from having the time of our lives.

I made some quick maneuvers, jumping rapidly across four stacks of marble, which I felt sure would confuse Scooter, looking up from below. When I laid down on one of the top slabs and peeked over the edge, he was nowhere to be seen and I thought I had fooled him. A moment later I heard him yelping and barking from what seemed to be a great distance away.

I jumped down onto a lower stack of marble and then again jumped about a dozen feet to a pile of soft earth and began looking for him. To my surprise I found that he wasn't very far away at all. He had just been barking while under one of the bottom slabs, which muffled his bark and gave the impression that he was farther away.

He was aggressively digging and barking under this slab, so I got on my hands and knees to see what he was after. I knew feral cats often had their kittens under the slabs, so it did not surprise me to see the silhouette of a cat back in the dark, under the slab, near to where Scooter was. I egged him on by saying, "Get him, Scooter, get him, boy."

Now, before you think me an insensitive wretch or cat hater, please let me explain. Scooter was all bark. He always had been. I knew it and he knew it. He was a very fast dog. He had often chased cats and rabbits through our yard, and usually caught them. And when he did, he would stop, back off, and sit there not knowing what he was supposed to do next.

He apparently knew that chasing cats was what dogs did best, but I guess no one ever explained to him why. His modus operandi was to chase, jump, and hold them down, then back off and watch them. He never bit them, never growled, never barked (except before the chase). He just seemed to like to chase them. Unfortunately for him, usually when he backed off, the victim cats would give him a quick swipe with their claws before making their escape. Even then, Scooter did nothing.

So, knowing this, I had no reservations egging him on. After doing so, I maneuvered myself to the place I thought the cat would exit when Scooter successfully flushed him out so I could catch him. Before I knew what was happening, the "cat" popped out from the darkness and, right before my eyes, transformed itself into a skunk—and a very angry one at that. I had no time to react. Scooter came shooting out of the hole behind the skunk at the same time I was choosing a quick escape route, while trying hard not to get bit by the skunk.

I think I might have made it, too, except for Scooter. He jumped on the skunk in his normal way and, to be honest, I don't really remember what happened next, except to say that the immediate area was enveloped in a rather sickening cloud of skunk musk.

The only experience I have ever had that came close to that nauseating day was going through the gas chamber at Navy Recruit Training. But at least a quick shower took the gas residue off. Not so skunk gas. Everything you see in the cartoons is true.

Your eyes burn, your skin burns, your face burns, and you cannot breathe without gagging.

You have to scrub yourself raw and when you are done doing that, you have to scrub again. Your clothes are permanent casualties and throwing them out is an option, but burying them is a better one. If you have long hair, kiss it good-bye as well. And finally, you must scrub again.

Scooter and I both learned a valuable lesson that day. I cannot speak for Scooter, but I know I never forgot it. There is a big difference between kitties and skunks!

DUKE THE DANGEROUS

As was common among career military families back in the 1950s and '60s, money was scarce and so was adequate housing. When your family uprooted because your father was transferred to a new duty station, it was fairly certain that it would be several months before you occupied your own semi-permanent residence again and life returned to normal.

The good thing about military life, however, and in particular the submarine service that my father was a part of, is that you generally traveled in the company of people you were stationed with before. Usually the entire crew and boat moves at the same time, at least in those days.

There exists camaraderie among sailors and their families that you just don't see in the everyday structure of our society. As shipmates, sailors become almost completely dependent on each other at sea. Some provide the meals, others the medicine, still others navigate the ship through dangerous waters while you sleep. There is great mutual trust and dependence.

That trust builds during the long, arduous months at sea, and sailors become close friends. This closeness is carried home to the families, who in turn grow closer to other families as they support each other in the absence of their sailors.

Within the families of men and women who wear dolphins on their uniform (devices that tell all they meet that they are submariners), there exists such a closeness that it is sometimes hard to tell where one family leaves off and another begins. They depend on each other for child care, transportation, and even lodging when times are tough. Often during the times of family transfer, homes of shipmates are opened to accommodate those in transit and their families. Dogs, cats, goldfish, and whatever else comes with the family are welcomed into the homes of shipmates who are already established in a household at the new duty station. It is not an inconvenience to have shipmates staying with you; it is a way of life.

Such was the case in 1959 when my father was reassigned to the submarine base in Groton, Connecticut. Housing was hard to get and money was very tight. Some wonderful shipmates opened their small home to us for several weeks. Dad, Mom, my sister, brother, grandmother, myself, and the cat all were welcomed. It was awkward and crowded, but a spirit of "can do" prevailed as shipmate helped shipmate.

While living with these selfless folks, I felt compelled to do whatever I could do to express my family's gratitude. Daily I cleaned and kept the entire house orderly. I cleaned bathrooms, made beds, ran errands, and took out the trash. I also volunteered to walk their dog.

I wanted to make their lives as comfortable as I possibly could to offset the inconvenience of my family's presence in their home. I know I was only a preteen and that responsibility was not mine, but I just felt burdened to do so. But I was not prepared for what walking the dog entailed.

Their dog was a large grayish-brown boxer named Duke. He was everything you would expect a boxer named Duke not to be. When I first heard his name, it conjured up visions of John Wayne and I was prepared for a stately, strong-willed stallion of a dog. He was far from living up to that expectation, however. He looked like a boxer, with that noble stance that boxers have. He held his head high and looked every bit the centurion of the premises. But looks certainly can be deceiving.

The woman of the house took me on my break-in walk with Duke. She said there were certain "things" I had to do. I did not give much thought to that comment because I knew dogs, and whatever things went along with the walk, well I was just the boy to handle it.

She put Duke on a leash and asked me to follow her outside. As we were walking, she explained that Duke had some very chronic ailments that made him sickly and weak. I would find out later that the gentleman of the house, a rugged old sailor, didn't like the dog for exactly the same ailments that I was about to learn about.

We had not gone very far, when the dog began his business. I noted that he had a very profound case of the runs (I wish there were a nicer way to put that). She explained that this was a side effect of his medications.

When he had completed his business, instead of scratching up the turf as most dogs do, he turned himself backward to the woman, who took a handful of tissues from her pocket and wiped her dog. That's love.

I was shocked. At my tender age I had never seen anything quite so shocking. I looked around to see if anyone was watching. I was embarrassed. No one wipes a dog, for goodness sake. I fought back the urge to tell her that perhaps I had been too hasty in offering to walk her dog. Instead, when she asked if I had any reservations in performing this job, I politely answered, "No, ma'am."

I was lying. I had a *big* problem. I did my job for a couple of days. I treated the dog as if he were an invalid. I wiped him. I hated every moment of it, but I wiped him. Eventually, I came to my wit's end. I had performed my last wipe and I was not going to wipe again. This dog was pitiful and I was going to make a man out of him—so to speak.

I began by walking him near the garden hose. When he needed wiping, he got washed. He didn't like that very much, but there wasn't much he could do. Then, to dry him off, I made him run. I actually had to teach him how to run. It was like a light went on in his head . . . "You mean, I can run?" He ran and jumped as if he had just been let out of prison. He was excited and from somewhere deep inside a flood of energy erupted from that dog. We went from my dragging him, to his running alongside, to his dragging me.

I was getting so worn out keeping up with him that I decided to take him off the leash. My goodness, it was like he turned into super dog. He ran around the courtyard of the apartments at a lightning pace, greeting everyone he encountered with a wagging of that stubby little tail that boxers have. I swear when he greeted them, he smiled and I knew it was his way of telling everyone "Look at me, look at me, I am alive." He stayed only a second before heading to the next person. It was like his coming-out party and he was taking his bows.

He came back to me in a sweat each and every time and we would re-leash and walk back to his house. He was so much more lively and energetic now. Coincidentally, as soon as his running started, his runs stopped.

The second week, I took Duke to a pond down in the cow pasture behind the apartment complex. We chased frogs and snakes and even fish. He learned how to enjoy mud and water, the way boys were supposed to. We went to the pond every day after that. It was the high time of our day. I would have to wash him with the garden hose and dry him off before we got home, or the pond smell would surely give us away.

One day at the pond, the cows moved in to water. They were everywhere, perhaps forty or fifty. They walked right up on us and bullied us out of the way. They were making it clear to us that the pond belonged to them and they wanted us to move. We just wanted our little part of the pond, but when we tried to go there, the cows would turn and face us as if they were prepared to defend it from our intrusion. They may have been bluffing, but I wasn't going to push it.

One of the cows made a halfhearted move toward us to scare

us off and Duke growled. I had never heard him growl before. This gave me an idea. I pointed at the cows and said, "Sic 'em, Duke." I wasn't expecting much reaction, but to my surprise Duke took off barking and charging the cows like he had been doing it all his life.

The cows apparently were as surprised as I was, reacting in concert to this unexpected aggression, fleeing no doubt for what they thought was their lives. Duke was unbelievable. He had that pond cleared of cows in less than thirty seconds. The whole herd was on the run. I was dumbfounded. I had made a monster out of the dog, and I was glad. In fact, I was proud. Duke had graduated. He was a real dog now, and he knew it, too. He came back with his chest puffed out and a different air about him. And it wasn't just the swamp algae hanging from his face that made him look tough. He had arrived!

Now when I walked Duke, he pulled me on the leash and walked proudly. He barked at every other dog he saw as if to say, "You aren't going to laugh at me anymore."

No one back at the house knew what Duke and I had been up to. I went to great pains to keep Duke under control and looking like his old self while in the house. It went rather well, until a knock came on the door one evening.

Duke heard the knock and went absolutely ballistic, barking and jumping and carrying on. This was something he had learned all on his own. Perhaps it is just something dogs naturally do. Whatever the reason, it took me as much by surprise as it did everyone else.

When he charged the door and made such a fuss, I thought

for sure the woman of the house was going to have a heart attack. She clutched her chest and stood there speechless. The only way I can describe it is to say she had a look of terror on her face. Something bad had happened to her Duke and she was visibly shaken.

She focused her eyes on me and it appeared she had almost instantaneously figured out that I was the cause for this awful display she was seeing in Duke. I was sure she was about to say something, when to my relief, her husband jumped out of his easy chair and said, "What on earth has come over that dog?" And then, reaching down to Duke on the back, he added, "Good boy, good boy."

To be honest, I don't remember if the door was ever answered. I was too busy holding my breath to see what kind of trouble I was in. When the smoke had cleared (Duke settled down), the husband wanted to know what had happened. He was apparently very pleased with the dog that now stood before him.

I explained in detail what we had been up to, leaving out anything that I thought would get me in trouble, such as chasing the cows. I told them of the running and the pond. I told them the diarrhea had stopped. I told them that even the other dogs in the neighborhood now gave Duke wide berth.

The woman was horrified. She cried. But the man laughed out loud and thanked me. He patted me on the back and said, "Things are going to be different around here for me and Duke from now on."

FUJI AND THE BUG

We had a solid black Siamese cat named Fuji who was quite the character. By necessity, he was an outdoor cat and that suited him just fine. He was a tough guy tom and liked to roam, quarrel with other toms, and just cause general unrest with the other neighborhood cats.

He also enjoyed the woods where we lived in Connecticut. He became very familiar with his surroundings and very comfortable, as well. He would go hunting into the woods and bring back little presents, which I will not discuss in detail here. Cat people know what I mean.

Somewhere near his third birthday, we were reassigned to Miami. We packed up and moved and quickly settled into our new home there. Fuji had no trouble making the physical adjustment to the more tropical environment. It was a bit hotter and more humid, but he seemed to adjust very well. But there were dangerous differences that neither of us had anticipated.

One morning, I saw him playing with what looked like a large insect. He often did this, so I was not too concerned. He caught cockroaches and those large palmetto bugs and toyed with them until he tired of it, as cats are inclined to do. Something about this insect seemed different, however, and I moved closer to get a better look. I immediately recognized the creature he held in his paws as a scorpion. As a younger child I had lived in Key West and had many experiences with them, including a scorpion farm I used to keep in the outside shed until my mother discovered it. I can still hear her screaming.

208 STORIES OF HUMOR

Fuji was swatting the insect back and forth like a hockey puck and the critter was becoming extremely agitated. Having been stung myself, I knew their wallop, so I moved as quickly as I could to try to stop the inevitable. Had I thought my action out a bit more, I probably would have opted to approach Fuji more slowly and soothingly. Instead, I hurried my movement and that caused him to think I was attempting to steal his newfound "toy." He pounced on the scorpion, picking it up in his mouth to run off. The now-angry scorpion thrust his weapon, but somehow missed Fuji's face, sinking his stinger deep into Fuji's upper shoulder.

Fuji did at least a triple somersault with a one-and-a-half twist, landed on all fours, and began wailing like only a Siamese can. He sounded just like a baby crying, but with an unearthly twang to it. Then, he headed straight up the nearest scrub pine.

If you are not familiar with scrub pines, they are unique trees in that they have no branches until you are about to the top of the tree. They grow almost perfectly straight and top out at about fifty or sixty feet. The branches start at about forty to forty-five feet. Fuji went straight up the tree without stopping until he reached the upper branches about fifty feet off the ground.

I was upset because I knew he could die if he had received too much venom. A person who does not have an allergy to the venom can take a sting and it is not much worse than a wasp, but a smaller animal can be overwhelmed by the toxin. I wanted to get him to a veterinarian as soon as possible, but there was just no way of getting him down. Climbing the tree would require a primate. Cutting it down would pose a greater risk to his life. And the fire department would not come.

So we waited. And we waited. We called out to him and tried to coax him down, but he would not come. So we waited. And we waited. That stubborn cat sat in that tree all day and into the night. I checked on him several times during the night and he was still up there. In the morning I tried again, but he would not move. I concentrated hard to see if I could detect movement. I was afraid he had passed away on the branch. But every so often he would wag his tail.

For three days and nights he sat in that tree. Eventually he turned his head and looked down at us when we called up to him, but he would not move. By this time I realized he was out of danger from the venom, but now I was worried about him never coming down. Finally, on the fourth day, we heard him crying at the door. I quickly grabbed him and hugged him and gave him the once-over. His arm was still swollen, so swollen in fact that he looked like he had been pumping weights. It was puffed up to make him look like the feline Charles Atlas.

He made a full recovery and became his same old self. I never saw him playing with bugs again, though. And somehow I think he missed Connecticut.

MIKO'S SWAN SONG

It is my opinion that some of the best animals you come by are those without pedigree. I am not putting down those animals that have papers, only underscoring the potential of those that do not. We acquired a "mutt" in the conventional sense of the word. She was a mixture of so many breeds, we stopped counting.

But that was not a detriment in any way. She was one of the most intelligent and energetic dogs we ever shared our lives with. Her name was Miko. She was an extraordinary animal.

Miko

Miko loved to swim. Her first introduction to water was at my mother's house in New Jersey. Mom had a pool with a wooden platform surrounding it. While I was swimming one day, Miko came up the ladder to see what I was doing. I coaxed her into the water over my mother's protests. At first she sort of inched her way over the edge to see what it felt like, but in one quick movement, she jumped right in. The jump was similar to that of a Jack Russell terrier. Perhaps that was one of her many mixes.

She swam to me, then around the pool awhile, splashing with her paws as she doggy-paddled, trying to catch the water her paws splashed up at the same time. I showed her the stairs and she climbed right out. I thought she was through, but she went back to the place she had first entered the pool and jumped right in again. She did not even stop to shake herself off as dogs usually do.

She continued jumping in, swimming to the ladder, running back to the entry point, and jumping in again. I tired of the water and wanted her to stop. The problem was, she did not want to. She had found something she really liked and she wasn't about to give it up. She was a water junky! So, employing my superior intellect, I put her back down on the ground and removed the only ladder leading to the platform. She went through some minor withdrawal pains, but she survived.

No too long after this, we were walking Miko in a small park. There was no one else around, so we decided to take her off her leash and let her run. We had forgotten her addiction to water. Wouldn't you know that she headed straight for the little pond in the corner of the park?

She stopped and looked at the water for a moment, as if she was wondering why it had no platform and was bigger than the pool she remembered. Then, before I could react, she picked out a huge boulder on the shore that extended out into the water, jumped up on the rock, and plunged right in. She then swam ashore, ran back to the rock, and jumped in again. She had not forgotten her experience at my mother's house.

None of us had noticed a big white swan swimming nearby. The swan was apparently coming over to see about the commotion. For those of you who are not familiar with the habits of swans, they are very territorial. Their looks are very deceiving . . . they make formidable aggressors. Miko had not seen the swan at first, but as it moved closer to the rock, the movement caught her attention. Miko looked hesitatingly at the bird, then back at me, then back at the bird, and then jumped in and started after it.

She reached the swan in pretty good time, but I do not think the encounter went quite as Miko expected. The crafty swan had slowly inched farther out into the pond, allowing Miko to reach it only when it was sure it had the advantage. It was not afraid of the dog, only stacking the deck in its favor. Miko barked wildly as she swam, and I could tell that she was tiring because her bark was labored. I was sure that I would have to dive in and rescue her soon.

The swan waited patiently for Miko to be far enough from shore that she could not easily escape and then it made its move. It swam quickly to my dog, so quick that it startled Miko. I am sure in her mind she was thinking Hey, things I chase aren't supposed to chase me. It was obvious that Miko had misjudged the situation. The bird was a lot bigger close up, not at all like those pigeons she chased earlier.

The bird started pecking at Miko's head and buffeting her with its large wings, trying to push Miko's head under the water to drown her. I heard Miko yelp out loudly as she turned to flee to shore. It was clear that she was willing to forget the whole matter . . . she would leave the pond if the darn bird would just leave her alone. But it wouldn't.

That swan beat Miko up pretty badly, biting and pecking on the almost defenseless dog all the way to the shore. Miko swallowed enough water to satisfy her need to jump in that pond ever again.

I was happy that I did not have to go in to rescue Miko, but a little angry at myself for letting the situation get out of control. As she climbed out of the water with her tail between her legs, I thought maybe this had been for the best. Miko had made it to shore a little worse for the wear, but a whole lot wiser in the things of the world. She would never make that mistake again. In fact, on subsequent walks to that park, she would not venture near that pond. There were too many swans there to know which one had taken Miko to school, but I am sure whichever one it was puffed out its chest feathers a little bit more each time Miko walked by.

SAMANTHA AND THE MYSTERY DOG

While stationed in Miami, my family and I occasionally enjoyed fishing in the mud flats of the Florida Bay off the Florida Keys. One particular area that I favored was just south of Marathon Key, a little northwest of the famous seven-mile bridge that exits Marathon heading south to Key West. A string of mangrove islands offshore in that area is popular with the local fish population. I have caught bonefish, tarpon, barracuda, sharks, snappers, and a host of other fish in these areas.

On one of our trips, it was exceedingly more hot than usual. The wind was calm and it was summer. You know the old question, "Is it hotter in the summer or in Miami?" The answer is "Miami." We had a boat with a bimini top, which protected us from the sun above, but the glare from the water negated the effects shade usually has.

Samantha

We had been swimming in the flats. I love to swim when the water looks like glass and it is between tides. There is no need to anchor the boat during such times for there is absolutely no wind or water movement. The water is like a large window to a beautiful world of color and life.

There we sat in the boat eating lunch, sitting motionless a few dozen yards from an atoll shaped mangrove island. It was hot, but still very enjoyable. My wife and children sat eating and drinking cold sodas, contemplating where we would motor to next, while I alone braved the sizzling sun and stood on the bow searching for fish or conch shells. Apparently, they too had sought the shade, for there were none to be seen.

To be fair, I wasn't the only one who was braving the sun. My trusted West Highland white terrier, Samantha (pictured on the cover), was in her normal position, standing right next to me. She was panting and very uncomfortable because of her thick coat. Thankfully, because it was white the fur did not absorb as much heat. Nevertheless, she was obviously hot. But nothing I could say would make her leave my side.

As she stood on her hind legs with her front paws on the railing of the boat, one of the many large birds in the mangrove trees on the island moved and this caught her attention. Because from our distance the white birds looked more like blossoms on the green mangrove branches, she wasn't sure what she had seen. But ever the vigilant guard, she felt she had to give at least a cursory, halfhearted bark.

The mangrove trees were so thick that they immediately bounced the sound back toward the boat. The echo of her bark startled her. She apparently thought there was a dog on the island. She quickly jumped up on the railing and let out a more emphatic bark, which in short order came back to her more emphatically. By now, Samantha's hair was standing up on her back and she was agitated. She was barking rapidly now and because echoes do not wait, they, too, came back rapidly.

Well, the whole thing was getting out of hand. Samantha was now running up and down the rail of the boat barking feverishly. She looked like she was going to jump in and swim to the island. My family and I were laughing so hard at the whole spectacle that we probably could have done nothing to prevent her. And I really did not want to go to the island to get her because in the depths of the mangroves live hordes of hungry mosquitoes.

Somehow Samantha managed to restrain herself from jumping in, and my wife and I regained our composure enough to retrieve her from the side rail. She wouldn't let it go, however. As we motored away to another island, she jumped up on the bow and continued to bark. Only when we were far enough away that there was no longer an echo did she stop. I am sure that in Sam's mind, she was the victor, having chased off that mysterious intruder.

THE HORSES OF GUANTANAMO BAY

During my years in the navy, as I think any seagoing sailor can claim, our ship made several trips to Guantanamo Bay, Cuba, more affectionately known as GTMO (pronounced gitmo). Here ships and crews undergo extensive testing for seaworthiness and proficiency, usually on an annual basis.

During one of these periods, I was given the day off for having worked so hard at my job. At least that is what they told me. So, I was to spend the day ashore while my aircraft carrier left port without me. This was unusual, but since I seldom took advantage of liberty in ports away from home, I decided it might be fun.

Thinking back now, I still wonder why this unusual and unique opportunity was extended to me. Usually you get foul-ups off the ship during important inspections. I was not a "foul-up." In fact, I received many accolades for my contributions and leadership. I was an important member of the operations division and it just didn't make sense that they were sailing without me. At the time it did not bother me, but now, many years later, I've changed my mind.

Could it be that they just did not want the inspectors to see me? I think that was it. The inspectors were the same people from the previous year and we had had a rather memorable moment during their last visit. I had inadvertently, and quite innocently, injured the chief inspector, a captain (O-6 in the navy) whose name now escapes me.

What happened was really just a fluke. The good captain wanted to check certain operational files to ensure that we were keeping them as prescribed. As he announced his desire, he stepped forward, positioning himself directly in front of the filing cabinets. As he stepped forward, he also pointed to the bottom drawer of the cabinet. Naturally, I thought this was the drawer he wanted opened, so I jumped to it rather smartly and pulled open the sliding drawer.

Apparently, he was one of those individuals who use their fingers to read, so what I perceived as his selecting the bottom drawer was in fact just his pointing at the drawer to read the label. As I turned to open the drawer, I had no way of knowing that he had quickly scanned the other drawer labels and decided he wanted to look in the top drawer. As you might imagine, as he stepped to retrieve the top drawer, I flung the bottom drawer open in smart military fashion.

The chief inspector did a very good job of controlling the volume of his expressed agony, but little could be done to keep his dignity after a bonehead stunt like that. Everyone in the room had witnessed what had happened. I had responded as any good sailor would. I knew it. The chief inspector knew it. Everyone knew it.

He grimaced a bit longer and rubbed his ankle, but said nothing about the incident. He then completed his task and left. He was very gracious about the whole thing. Unfortunately, it still came up in our critique of the trials and I caught a few "ribbings" about it. I think one of the comments was, "Hey Gary, I heard you know how to 'drawer' out the best in captains."

So, if my absence from the ship was by design, it was to keep from reminding the inspectors of the previous year's fiasco. Still, I doubt that was the reason, because several sailors from other ships had also been let off for the day and those I spoke with said that they had also been selected for a day off as a reward for their good work. Could it be that I was not alone in my history of inspector assault, or had the admiral really decided to give a day off to one person on each ship for outstanding work? I suppose I will never know, but I prefer to believe the latter.

That was not the humorous story I wanted to tell. That was only the background for setting up the story. Once on the island, I encountered several men from the other ships at one of the few attractions on the base, the livery stables. Here you could rent a horse for an hour tour around an established trail.

The stables contained about a dozen horses, all of which were reported to give quiet, soothing rides around the marked course. I thought this would be a good diversion. More important, it was cheap. The horses were good-looking creatures, well fed and well padded. They reacted very well to petting and appeared friendly enough. So, we paid our money and chose our animals. We then departed on a journey I have never forgotten.

I cannot say for sure how long the course was, but certainly it was not very long, perhaps between one-quarter and one-half mile. We started out with the horses walking at a slow pace and then picked it up to a faster walk. We hadn't gotten 200 feet from the barn, however, when the horses came to a grinding halt. Not one of them, but all of them . . . almost as if by command.

We encouraged them repeatedly to move forward and after about twenty minutes, we had only gained about the same amount of footage. A foot a minute seemed to be a little unsatisfactory to me. The trail was clearly marked and well traveled and I could not understand why my horse did not want to go. I dismounted and pulled on the reins, dragging him along. The horse actually pulled back on me in rebellion and gave me that white-eyed look horses give when they don't agree with you.

Having some experience with horses, I decided to show him who was boss and I bullied him along for another hundred feet or more, until I tired. I did not hurt the animal. I only took charge and let him know that I could be as stubborn as he. The other fellows were having similar problems, but they were far behind me now and I really lost interest in anything else around me. My whole being, my whole purpose, was to ride this horse. It was me and this stubborn, unreasonable animal, alone in the world, locked in a battle of the wills.

I tried everything. I was kind. I spoke sweet nothings in his ear. I bribed him. I pulled grasses up for him to eat. None of that had any positive effect. I changed tactics. I yelled. I screamed. I cried. I tried embarrassing him. I told him he was shameful. Nothing worked, nothing but pulling.

And so I pulled, and pulled, and pulled, for the next forty-five minutes. Inch by inch we made our way out, around and back on that trail. By the time I had gotten to where I could see the barn again through the trees, I was a soiled sweating mess. I had human sweat on top of horse sweat on top of dirt from pulling up grass. I was disheveled and dirty and I smelled like a horse. I was worn out and tapped of all energy. But he was moving! And that was what this was all about after all. I was winning! Wasn't I?

I don't know where the marker was, but somewhere after we cleared the trees and we could see the barn clearly, that horse suddenly came to life and took off like a bolt of lightning. He didn't warn me. He didn't even give me a hint. He saw his stable and that was that. He jerked me clear off the ground and dragged me down the remainder of the path. I had never understood the term "he smelled the barn" until I actually saw it in action.

I was not only exhausted, but now I was humiliated. And as I tried to dust off the humility with the dirt, the stable hand asked, "Did you have a good ride?" He knew I hadn't. He knew no one ever did. He was in cahoots with the horses. Together their job was to take money from sailors and then strip them of their dignity.

No doubt he had heard me bragging earlier that I had been on horses before and learned from the Blackfoot Nation how to handle them. No doubt he knew just what scam artists those horses were. And no doubt he wanted to teach me a lesson. But I wasn't going to give him the satisfaction. Sore and worn, sweaty and smelly, I mustered whatever pride I had left and answered, "Oh it was the best, thanks."

BEARING IT ALL AT THE
COAST GUARD ACADEMY

During one of my tours in the United States Coast Guard, I was assigned to the staff of the superintendent, U.S. Coast Guard Academy in New London, Connecticut. I was the senior member of the Academy Special Security Force. My duties included supervising twenty other security personnel in special functions that demanded crowd control, parking assistance, automobile searches, funeral details, and other undesirable duties that our regular security force didn't feel like doing.

One morning in 1981 I received a telephone call ordering me to organize my special security force for a special assignment. I notified my force and told everyone to arrive in Service Dress Blues, the uniform of the day, with full security gear and helmets.

When I arrived, I asked the officer of the day what the special assignment was and was told that the academy mascot, a 100-pound northern black bear, had escaped from his pen. He was creating havoc in the community surrounding the Academy, that is, turning over trash cans, scaring children and dogs, and so on. My job was to recapture the mascot. Needless to say, no one was happy that we were going to have to accomplish this task in our dress uniform, myself included . . . but we had no time to change.

Knowing that bears usually return to their den after rummaging, I figured he would come back to the academy grounds and his cage. It was the only place familiar to him. I posted people at strategic locations believing they would be there for a very long time waiting on the bear. To my surprise, within fifteen minutes the bear was spotted back on campus. We organized ourselves by radio and converged on that location.

The bear immediately figured out what our intentions were and broke for the football field, probably the area best known by a campus mascot. Once there, he made fools of us, running in and out of bleachers, around the press box, and finally under the bleachers.

I was not sure what to do at this juncture as there was not much more than crawl space under that section of bleachers and it was very dark and very wet. About the same time, a good friend of mine, the only force member I was not able to locate, came walking out of the enlisted club. He had obviously been drinking (he was off duty) and was "feeling good," if you know what I mean.

He asked, "What's going on, Gary?" I explained and then added, "But we have it under control, why don't you just go sleep it off?" I returned to the problem at hand and forgot about my friend, thinking he would follow my advice. I don't know how he managed it, but before I knew what was going on, he had crawled under the bleachers and toward the bear.

I kneeled down and tried to see back up in the dark shadows of the bleachers, but I was not able to discern any of the shapes. I was able to hear, however. My inebriated friend had apparently not located the bear yet, for he was calling loudly, "Here kitty kitty kitty." The entire security force broke out in hysterical laughter at this drunken display of bravado. We were in stitches and in danger of losing all objectivity, when we were brought back to reality by a loud growl and my friend's scream. We learned later that he had found the bear, grabbed its stub tail, and the bear had retaliated with a quick bite on the hand.

Almost simultaneously with the scream, that rascal bear came darting out from under the bleachers, heading for the lower football field. His way was blocked, however, because as we had anticipated he might bolt and had surrounded the immediate area. As soon as he realized that he was outnumbered, he scurried up the nearest tree. And as you might guess, it was not one of the smaller ones.

A few moments later the state Fish and Game Commission agents arrived on scene. I had summoned them earlier in case we needed to tranquilize the bear. To my chagrin, they did not come with the tranquilizing equipment, explaining that they did not have access to it on the weekends. I wondered out loud, but under my breath, why they had come at all. But they wanted to help and I welcomed their expertise in capturing wild animals.

That welcome was short-lived. Their first (and only) plan was one I did not support or condone. Briefly, they wanted someone to climb up the tree and tie a rope off at about twenty feet below the fifty-foot mark where the bear had decided to sit. The idea was to tie the rope to their truck and shake the tree back and forth, scaring the bear into coming down. I protested, but they assured me this was a tactic that always worked. So I temporarily turned the mission over to them. One of them climbed up and tied off the rope on the tree. Then they tied the rope to the bumper of the truck. They began their plan of rocking the tree back and forth. A short lunge of the truck forward, then throwing the transmission into neutral and being pulled back a bit, then again in drive. The tree shook and, amazingly, the bear actually did begin to stir. In fact, he moved down the tree a foot or two. A few more shakes and the bear started on his way down. He definitely did not like the tree shaking.

When he reached the thirty-five-foot mark, for some reason he decided to head back up the tree. The men from the state overreacted to this change of plans and hit the gas a little too hard. The tree bent to the point of almost breaking, but the rope gave way first.

The tree, now free from the rope's tautness, was transformed into a catapult. That poor bear was thrown some fifteen feet through the air and forty feet down. I cringed. I thought the little guy was history. To my amazement, he hit the ground on all fours, never missing a step, and he was off to the races.

He was past me before I realized that he had weathered the fall. I started off right behind him, in full dress uniform with my utility belt, handcuffs, and billy club flopping around. My helmet was bouncing around on my head, giving me the appearance of the head on one of those hula-girl dolls people put on the dashboards of their cars. Lumbering down the trail through a small patch of woods, I chased after that bear all the way to the softball and soccer fields of the lower campus.

I was surprised at the speed of this small creature. He was less than twenty-four inches high on all fours, but his feet seemed to never touch the ground. I knew bears were fast, but I never suspected they were able to put on bursts of speed like this. I was right behind him, though, shedding my cumbersome gear and jacket as I ran. I thought by lightening my load I would be able to catch up to him, but that proved to be yet another miscalculation on my part. Despite my speed increase, he managed to keep the same distance between us.

He arrived at the lower field ahead of me, but rather than entering the field, he turned south on the railroad tracks that transit the lower campus. This was a break for me because the spaces between the railroad ties proved a hindrance to him. So I poured it on and finally managed to pull alongside him.

I threw all my weight into him trying to knock him off the track and getting him to roll. It had little effect, except that I lost some ground. I again came alongside him and this time tackled him. We both rolled off the tracks and onto the shoulder of the track mound. I recovered from the roll faster than he and I pounced on his back. I knew that as a 200-pound weightlifter, I would be able to control this smaller 100-pound youngster.

This was yet another miscalculation. He got up on all fours with me square on his back and my arms around his neck, and started running toward the adjacent cyclone fence. I could not believe the power of this small animal. About this time, four other men arrived and jumped on my back. They had been laboring to catch up to us carrying a large volleyball net they thought might come in handy. Before jumping on my back, they threw this net over the bear and me.

We had him now, or so we thought. That stubborn bear continued moving toward the fence carrying all five of us on his back. We must have presented at least half a ton of weight, yet he was able to stand and move. He dragged us about a dozen more feet and was finally stopped only because he tried to climb under the fence and got his head stuck. Otherwise, I am not sure we would have held him.

We took advantage of the situation. While he struggled with the fence, we began wrapping the net around him to contain him. Someone thought to bring the academy ambulance on scene. It probably was brought in the event someone needed to be treated, but as it turned out, we used it to transport the bear.

I know it sounds ridiculous, but the now twenty people on scene could not handle that little fireball of a bear. I made the decision to take everything, the bear, the net, and me, and throw us in the back of the ambulance and ferry us over to the bear's large cage. Somehow, as this tangled mass was lifted into the ambulance, I was fortunate enough to slide out just before the doors slammed shut.

It actually proved to be the easiest part of the entire event. Everything went relatively smoothly, considering what we had previously gone through, and we all finally had a chance to relax. Our guard was let down too prematurely, however, as no sooner had the doors on the ambulance closed, than the bear commenced a terrible ruckus inside.

He was obviously trying to get himself out of the net, too. He thrashed around inside the ambulance, knocking over equipment and ripping things off the inner bulkheads. We learned later that he had bit holes in the cushions of the portable personnel carriers, among other things, and left deep scratch marks in the floor surface, presumably from trying to dig his way out. When we eventually opened the doors, we were stunned at what damage he had done. How could one little bear cause so much trouble?

We backed the ambulance right up to the edge of his cage. In the event he somehow broke our grip on him when we opened the ambulance, I wanted him to have no opportunity to go anywhere but into his cage.

This bear was not through surprising us, however. Now, with ambulance doors wide open, he decides that the ambulance he fought so hard to get out of wasn't that bad after all and he refused to leave. He backed up into a corner and started growling and snapping at our attempts to pull him out. He also tried to take swipes at us with his filed-down claws, but because the net was still wrapped around his upper torso, his range was hampered.

I know I will sound as if I am embellishing a bit, but that 100-pound bear fought off all our attempts to pull him out for about twenty minutes. Finally, in frustration, I mustered up my courage, jumped up in the ambulance, gathered up as much of the net as I could, flung it on top of him, and bear-hugged (if you will pardon the pun) the whole pile of net and bear. I quickly lifted the 150-pound bundle as I simultaneously turned toward the fence and half tossed, half carried everything over it, into his cage.

Almost everything went well. We (the bear and I) cleared the ambulance—the dangling portions of net did not get hung up on anything—I muscled everything over the fence without too much effort. *But*, as I did so, that rascal somehow reached through the net and sunk his ¾-inch teeth right into my rump. It hurt! It hurt a lot! There wasn't much damage to my pants—just a few puncture marks and a little blood, but the "pinch" of it stung badly.

After dropping the mesh of bear and net over the fence and

doing a little dance while rubbing the sting out of my posterior, I jumped the fence to untangle the bear. When he completely emerged from the net, he had this stupid grin on his face, almost a smile. He leaned over, licked my hand, and then ran to his water bowl for a drink as if nothing had happened. It was as if he were saying, "Hey, that was fun, let's do it again sometime."

The last I had heard was that the bear had grown to over 300 pounds. I was very thankful that I was no longer at that station.

MARCO ISLAND MAYHEM

This story is more for fathers, because I think they will understand.

My family and I drove to Marco Island from Miami to go fishing one Saturday morning. For those of you unfamiliar with Florida, Marco Island is in the southwest corner of the state near Naples. It is a rather ritzy neighborhood, and finding a place to fish proved difficult, but I finally found a vacant ocean-side lot. The water was beautiful, the day was beautiful, and my wife and two children were finally waking up from their ninety-minute nap (coincidentally the same amount of time it took me to drive there).

It was already getting hot, so the first order of business was to build a lean-to-type shelter for the wife and kids so they could escape the heat. I came prepared with tarps, ropes, a few boards, and, most important, a plan. So erecting the shelter only took about fifteen minutes—at least the first time.

Upon completion of the rather adequate makeshift tent, my

wife announced that the car (which was the base for my shelter) was facing in the wrong direction. As any good father would, I kept my cool, disassembled my shelter, moved the car, and started over. For some reason, perhaps because I was in a hurry to begin fishing, the shelter didn't have quite as much pizzazz as the previous version. No matter, it worked.

I then turned my attention to getting the fishing poles ready. They were in the trunk. Yes, you guessed it! In my haste I had secured the shelter to the tailgate of the car with a rope and now could not open the trunk. So, after yet another small adjustment, I had extracted the fishing gear and reattached the rope that held up the now wobbly shelter.

By this time the family had moved from the still running, air-conditioned car to the lounge chairs I had set up in the shade under the shelter. As I handed them the cool drinks they requested, it occurred to me that no one had bothered to turn off the car's engine. I took care of that small chore and began putting the fishing poles together and rigging them with sinkers and hooks. I made mental note that the sun was beginning to get a little warm.

Next, I found great locations for the pole holders and I hammered them into the ground. Unfortunately, I had forgotten my hammer and was forced to use a grapefruit-size stone instead. The numbness in my hand from inadvertently leaving it between the rock and the pole holder once too many times did not hamper my ability to cut the bait and put it on the hooks, however, so all was not lost.

"What's that, honey?" I called out to my wife who was saying something from under the shelter. I couldn't really hear her from where I was and I couldn't make out where she was sitting because of the contrast between the glaring hot sun and the shade of the cool shelter. But I knew she was under there somewhere, in the shade, near the cooler, with a nice cold drink in her hand.

When she repeated herself I heard her clearly and followed with, "Oh, yes I know it's hot, but you have that nice shade and the kids are going to have such a great time . . ." My voice trailed off as I realized she wasn't really listening. It didn't matter, because the real action was about to start as I picked up the first pole and started my first cast.

It was a perfect cast, right where I wanted it. I placed the pole in the holder and said to my ten-year-old daughter, "Tammy, that one is yours." Another pole, another great cast, and a big grin on my face as I told my son of fourteen, "Eric, this one is yours." "Okay, Dad," came their replies in unison.

No sooner had they acknowledged their pole assignments, than the first pole took a hit. My daughter raced out to pick up the pole and battle the fish. "Dad, I can't do it, it is too hard," she cried. Good dad that I am, I took the fishing pole from her and landed her catch. It was a three-pound sail catfish.

Releasing the fish, I turned to see my son reeling in his line. "Do you have one, son?" I asked. "No, Dad" was his reply, "I just wanted to check my bait." "Oh," said I outwardly, but screaming inwardly, "but I just put it out five minutes ago." After getting the sinker stuck in the coral three times (with me wading out to work it free) he reeled it in, saw that the bait was all there, and attempted to cast it out again.

Surely I was in a cartoon! A cast that bad only happens to Goofy. The dent in the car did not bother me quite as much as the bird's nest that he had created in the reel by not keeping thumb pressure on it. My son's adding "Well, at least I didn't lose the bait" didn't make matters better.

I decided to get both the daughter's and wife's poles out before I tackled (pardon the pun) the job of straightening out the line. That took me just a minute or two and I was back inspecting the bird's nest. "This should be a cinch!" I said out loud. It wasn't.

Fortunately, I had brought along extra line. And after cutting away the tangled blob that once was new line, I started spooling line back on the reel. Before I could complete that task, however, my wife called out from somewhere in the dark recesses of the shelter, "Honey, one of the poles has a bite." I looked, and indeed it did. Something big.

I grabbed the pole about the same time that I noticed my daughter reeling in her own pole. She had something, too! She had my wife's fishing line. Of course, when she realized she did not have a fish, she handed me her pole and retreated to the coolness of the shelter while I sorted out which line was which. This complete, I again cast both lines out and reset the poles. I then continued putting line on my son's reel.

For the next three hours, my pole sat on the ground. In fact, the line on my reel never did get wet that day. I spent all of my time bating, casting, catching, and removing from the hook all the "yucky" fish no one else wanted to touch. When I hooked and landed the biggest fish of the day on my wife's pole, and she said, "Wow, I guess I caught the biggest fish today," I knew it was time to go home. She had not so much as peeked out from

under the shelter while I hooked and landed the ten-pound creature, but somehow because it was her pole, she claimed the
achievement.

Totally worn out, I asked if everyone was ready to go. I ignored the "We didn't even want to come" comment and said,
"Well, I know it is hot, but we had a great time together didn't
we?" The lack of response and raised eyebrows ordinarily would
have hurt my feelings, but suddenly one of the poles bent over
double with line screaming off the reel.

I grabbed the pole as the family finally came out from under
the shelter and showed some enthusiasm. They gathered around
me and asked, "What is it, Dad, what is it?" I didn't know for
sure, but I had caught a lot of fish before and this one was big.
The way it was running, I felt sure it was a bull shark. The way
it was pulling I guessed it to be near a hundred pounds.

I had to be cautious. The tackle I was using was not made for
this big of a fish. I reached over and adjusted the drag on the
reel to allow less line to be pulled out, but not enough to cause
the line to break. No matter, the fish kept ripping line off the
reel.

I found myself inching closer and closer to the water just to
try to keep the big fish from emptying the reel. Finally, waist-
deep in the water and on the edge of a deep channel, the fish
slowed. Then he stopped. Then he started coming back!

I reeled in the slack line as quickly as I could, hoping he would
not throw the hook before I had the line taut. With the line finally tight again, I felt the fish still struggling, but still swimming back in my direction.

Suddenly, out of the corner of my eye I saw a dark shadowy

figure in the depths of the channel. Flashbacks from the movie *Jaws* quickly flooded my mind and the hair on the back of my neck stood up! Here I was in waist-deep water at the edge of the channel with an angry shark heading my way. What was I thinking?

Before I could react, the large figure came up from the depths headed right for me. My heart was in my throat. I dropped the pole and got ready for impact. I wasn't sure what I was going to do, but I wasn't going easy.

The head of the creature broke the surface not two feet from me and gently let out a gulp of air that sounded like "phfoooooo." It was a manatee. Though I was still shaken by the thought of almost being a meal, I reached over and patted the big lovable animal on the head. He submerged again and slowly disappeared into the deep.

I still had the shark on the line, but it turned out to be only around sixty pounds. He was about as exhausted as I was, so after pulling him in, I quickly took him out to deeper water and let him go.

I turned back toward my family and said, "Let's go home." No one argued. They even helped me take down the shelter. All the way home they talked about what a good time they had. For a moment I wondered if I had gotten in the right automobile.

THE SHADY COW

People who love animals are usually special people, the kind of people who make this world a better place to live in. They are caring and selfless, often sacrificing time and resources to ensure an animal has love and care. You will find these people at shelters cleaning cages, caressing the unwanted, feeding strays, and generally making it a better world for our furry and feathered friends. These are noble and much appreciated people.

Hidden within the ranks of these special people, however, are the elite "special forces" of animal lovers, the heroes. They earn this title with their willingness to go beyond helping out at shelters and on rescue projects. These types readily leave their comfort zone and take a risk in order to help an animal that appears to be in distress.

*The suffering of an animal becomes
personal to them.*

I am not talking about radical animal rights activists who violate the law and the rights of others. I speak rather of people who have no ulterior motive or political agenda except a heart swelling with love for animals. The suffering of an animal becomes personal to them. They cannot rest or concentrate until they at least try to do something positive for the creature at risk.

The best remedy for animal abuse, of course, is to lobby for local legislation that addresses and fixes the problem. Too often, a more immediate response is required to remove the danger to the animal. I am no hero and do not count myself among the ranks of those who are, but there was this one time when I simply had to take action.

It was in Houston and it was hot. I had just come out of a home improvement store, when I noticed a cow in the back of the store inside the caged lagoon. I found out later that the store rented this cow from a local rancher to keep the vegetation in the fenced area under control.

It was a good environment, enough room for the cow to roam, plenty of vegetation to eat and a constant, although questionable, water source. The one drawback was the lack of trees or structure to provide shade for the cow. On this particular day it was 107 degrees, a blistering day. The cow's dark color was rapidly absorbing the sun's heat and it just looked miserable. It was standing in the water to stay cool, but even that provided very little relief for the suffering animal.

Those of you who have been to Texas in the summer know how overwhelming the heat can be. I could not bear to see the cow suffer any longer. I immediately got on the phone and called the local chapter of the SPCA. The person who answered told me that the sheriff had jurisdiction, who told me that the county animal control office was the one to call, who informed me that the constable for that township had cognizance, who told me to contact the SPCA!

The wind had been taken out of my sails by all this political shuffle; but I was not beaten yet. I went to the store and asked the manager if he could do something and his response was very positive. "Sure, of course, we'll get right on that." Two days later nothing had been done and the poor creature was still suffering.

I contacted the sheriff again and was told quite sarcastically, "Cows and horses are not bothered by the hot summer sun . . . don't worry about it." Rebel that I am, I had to ask, "If that is true, why is it that all the other cows I see around here are under trees?" I will not record her response. Suffice it to say, it was a dead end. This woman was not an animal person. She didn't care.

Getting off my soapbox and back to the story, I still was not ready to cry "uncle." Early the next morning (about 4:00 a.m.), I drove over to that store and scaled the fence with a tarp and rope in hand. Okay, I know earlier I said I am not for breaking the law and trespassing is breaking the law, but I sincerely was not out to hurt anyone or any property. I just could not stand to know that animal was suffering.

After scaling the fence, I went to one of the corners of the fenced-in area and erected a shade tarp, fastening it to both the lines of fence that extended out from the corner. The cow stood there giving me a puzzled look, but I knew she would eventually appreciate my hard work. Finally she would have some relief.

I was so proud of what I had done. Each day I stopped by several times to see how the cow was doing, hoping to bask in my glory as she stood or rested under the shade I had erected. Oddly, each time I went, she was standing in the water or out in the hot sun.

Okay, the truth is that I never once saw her use the shade. I actually sat in my truck for over an hour during the hottest time of the day and she never once went anywhere near the shade. After a couple of weeks, the rain and wind knocked the tarp down and then she went over to smell it. There can be no denying the fact. That cow made a monkey out of me.

"THUMP, THUMP, THUMP"

While at Yellowstone National Park several years back, I some-how turned off on a road that apparently was not well known by tourists. We drove for several miles and did not see anyone. I am glad Americans flock to our national parks and enjoy them, but it was good to get away from the maddening crowd for a while and enjoy the peaceful part of the park that we had found.

It seemed less dangerous, too. An hour earlier, back with the big crowds, my wife had beckoned me to go down by some other tourists and take pictures of the colorful hot water springs. I stopped her and said, "Don't go down there, it is dangerous."

She gave me a puzzled look and asked, "Dangerous? How can it be dangerous—everyone else is down there?"

I responded, "Do you see that rock?" pointing down near where several men with cameras were standing.

She said, "Yes."

"Well," I said, "that is no rock. That is a bison. It only looks like a rock curled up on the ground in the shade."

She laughed and was about to express her doubt when the bison stood up and shook itself off. The men had gotten too close and it was not happy. Fortunately, it headed away from the men instead of toward them.

So I was happy to be away from tourists who really are not familiar with nature enough to know how to keep from provok-ing animals. This road we had found was just wonderful. There was no one around and we didn't have to deal with traffic jams due to everyone stopping to see a frog hopping across the road.

Okay, that is a slight exaggeration, but if you have visited a national park, you know what I mean.

We got out of the car at a very nice overlook. The sloping hills leading up to the overlook housed a colony of chipmunks, and we had a wonderful hour of just watching them run around chasing each other and socializing. It was such a nice diversion.

Suddenly, there was a twig-cracking sound that came up from the grove of trees far below us, which was perhaps sixty feet down from the lookout. My kids said, "What was that, Dad?"

I replied, "It could have been an elk stepping on a branch or a beaver cutting down a sapling, but to be honest, I think it was a bear scratching his back on a tree."

There young eyes lit up as they said "Bear?" I had only been joking with them. I actually thought it was probably an elk walking around. Suddenly, the unmistakable "growl" of a large bear came from the woods. I tried to concentrate to see if I could see the animal, but it was too dark in the thick woods.

I turned to my kids to say "See!" but they were not there. The "thump, thump, thump" of three car doors slamming shut told me that my one-word exclamation would have been wasted.

Daily Devotional: The Promises of God

The loss of a precious pet is often one of life's most traumatic experiences. Though we are surrounded with family and friends, we frequently feel as if we are alone in our grief and that no one understands what we are going through.

The first thirty days are understandably the most difficult to endure. The pain seems unbearable and the future looks dim, if you can think about it at all. Friends and family are trying to be supportive, but they just don't seem to understand the depth of your pain and how your life has been turned upside down. It seems the whole world around you has gone mad. They do not seem to realize or care what has happened to you.

This devotional is offered to show you that someone does care and that the way you feel is important to him. He wants you to know that He is in control and that the things that weigh heavily upon your heart can be lightened through trust in His promises.

The following daily entries are gleanings from both the Old and New Testaments. Please read them and apply them to your situation and life. Please discipline yourself to read only one entry each day for the next thirty days. Meditate upon the promise we discuss for that day to see how it applies to your life.

By reading a promise you are seeing what God has to say. By meditating on that promise, you are seeing what God has to say . . . to you. There is no trick in claiming the promises of God. It takes only faith and trust.

Day 1: The Promise of God's Presence

I will never leave you.
—Hebrews 13:5

In life, those we love can leave us. Children grow up and move on with their own lives. Spouses lose affection and separate or divorce. Friends move away. And of course, loved ones, human and animal, pass away.

Life is in a constant state of flux for us and we never know when things are going to change. Sometimes life can seem so unpredictable and unfair that we find ourselves wondering if anyone is really in control of it all.

Rest assured that someone is in control. When you are at your lowest, when you feel alone and broken, remember that God is aware of your situation. He says, *"I will never leave you."* It is His promise and when God makes a promise, He keeps it. His promises never fail.

As you deal with the grief of losing a cherished pet, remember his promise is that you are not alone. In your grief, he is there and he will not leave your side. He will dry your tears and lift you up. He will see you through these difficult times.

Day 2: The Promise of God's Protection

Fear not . . . I am thy shield.
—Genesis 15:1

While we can appreciate the beauty of our world and enjoy the wonders of life, the actual living of it can bring us some very hard emotional blows. It has been said that we may not always be able to control the things that happen to us, but we can control the way we react to them.

No doubt if we can control our reaction, we can limit the adverse impact that life's circumstances have upon us, but sometimes we are not able to find the "stuff" within ourselves to keep a positive and persevering attitude. Fortunately, our scripture for the day promises us that God has the stuff we need and He will be our shield from life's fiery darts.

The loss of a precious pet can be one of life's most traumatic and unsettling experiences. As we go through the arduous and lengthy recovery process, it is normal to wonder if our pain will ever subside. Indeed, because each new morning revives our pain, we can even develop a fear of facing the next day.

As this morning breaks, remember the encouragement in our scripture to *"fear not."* Through faith, allow the Lord to shield you from those fears. In time, He will shield you also from the pain.

Day 3: The Promise of God's Rest

Come unto me all ye that labor and are heavy
laden, and I will give you rest.
—Matthew 11:28

Let us focus on the "heavy laden" portion of today's devotional scripture. Emotions such as grief and sorrow are extremely heavy loads for anyone to carry. They lay hard upon our hearts and can make us feel so very alone.

This is especially true when we lose someone as close as a pet. While some may see pets as nothing more than another of life's responsibilities, most of us appreciate them as intimate friends with whom we share very personal joys and experiences. They are live-in confidantes who know the real us, but who cherish our friendship in spite of that knowledge.

When our best friend takes their leave of this world, the emotional burden is often more than we can bear. Others can sometimes appreciate what we are going through. They can express their best wishes and lend a modicum of support, but they can never take that burden away for us. Their intentions are pure, but their ability to help falls far short of our needs.

There is one who can help, however. The Lord promises to give us rest. If we will share our heaviness with him, he will take it upon himself and rest our hearts. We are reminded in scripture that he was "a man acquainted with grief" and we have the confidence of knowing that he understands what we are going through.

The burden of losing a friend as dear as a pet is very heavy indeed, one that no one should have to endure alone. Take a rest from your pain and heartache by sharing it with the Lord. Cast your burden upon him in prayer and let him carry it for you.

Day 4: The Promise to Provide

I will help thee.
—Isaiah 41:10

There are many accounts in scripture where it seemed all was lost for those in the story. Without the Lord's promise of help, and subsequent intervention, all might have indeed been lost.

Daniel was thrown into the lion's den and surely would have been torn to pieces if it were not for God's help. We are told *"but God sent an angel . . ."* and Daniel was not lost. In fact, not only did God help, but He turned the intended consequence around so that it fell upon the evil men who had purposed for Daniel to die rather than Daniel himself.

In another account we are told that Israel had been trapped between the forbidding Red Sea and the pursuing Egyptian army. There was no way for them to escape. All seemed lost, but again we read *"but God . . . ,"* and they were delivered.

As you face this new day with the pain of losing your best friend, it may seem to you like all is lost, that you are facing your own emotional lions and Red Sea. There is no denying that you are faced with a substantial change in your life and that it is going to be difficult to adjust. *"But God"* will help if you will place your trust in Him.

Day 5: The Promise to Hear

> *The righteous cry and the Lord heareth.*
> —Psalm 34:17

In this world of almost 7 billion people, it is hard to be noticed, much less heard. It seems you have to be a member of a special interest group or a celebrity of some sort to command any attention at all.

The promise for today guarantees that those who trust in the Lord have an audience with Him. Not only does He listen, but He responds with action. We saw this in yesterday's examples of the times when He was a help to those in need.

When the peace and happiness of the home is suddenly broken by the passing of a family pet, it seems that things will never get back to normal. The full water bowl sits untouched and unmoved. The toys that your best friend once played with are still scattered around the living room. There just seems to be no reason and no motivation to put things away. Often you just feel like screaming or crying out.

In time, your heart will heal, but you want help for today. May I suggest that if you are going to cry out, why not cry out to the Lord? He promises to hear. He promises to help. He promises to heal.

Day 6: The Promise That God Will Prosper

But my God shall supply all your needs.
—Philippians 4:19

Prosperity can mean more than financial increase and wealth. Sometimes good health, family, friends, a good church, and any number of things can be more precious than money. Though our hearts are heavy from a personal loss, our attitude should be one of thankfulness for the other precious things that God supplies.

The late Matthew Henry, scholarly theologian and commentator, was once attacked and mugged on a dark street. When asked for comments on his experience, he thoughtfully pondered what his response might be and then said, "I am thankful."

Seeing the puzzled look on the reporters' faces, he added, "I am thankful for four things. I am thankful that I had something worth robbing. I am thankful that while they took all that I had, it was not very much. I am thankful that while they robbed me of what I had, they did not rob me of my life. And most of all I am thankful that it was I who was robbed and not I who robbed."

Moving on in your life does not mean you leave your best friends behind. You can carry your pet in your heart and be thankful for the time you had. You can also be sure that God will supply your needs and give you many more things in your life to be thankful for. Your loss did not go unnoticed. He will supply your needs, whatever they may be.

Day 7: The Promise of God's Purpose

I know the thoughts that I think toward you . . .
thoughts of peace, and not of evil.
—Jeremiah 29:11

There are times when we feel our prayers go no higher than our bedroom ceiling, that they bounce right back at us, unheard and unanswered. Similarly, there are days when we wonder if God is even aware that we exist, let alone that He is concerned about how we feel and what we are going through.

In the very lowest of times, some even imagine that their calamity and woe is some sort of punishment from God. The disciples exhibited this type of thinking in John, chapter 9, when they asked the Lord about the cause of the blind man's ailment. They asked the Lord if he was blind as a result of his sin or his parent's sin. The Lord answered *"Neither, but that God might be glorified."*

It is human nature to think that somehow "what goes around comes around" and hardships and sufferings are a result of some wicked thing we did, some retribution from God. You may be thinking that the untimely loss of your pet is due to something you may have done or not done as the case may be. You might think that somehow life or fate or God has it in for you.

Nothing could be further from the truth. God's thoughts toward us are good and benevolent. The loss of a wonderful pet is precious in the sight of the Lord. He knows the pain you are enduring and wants you to know that His thoughts toward you are thoughts of peace, not evil.

Day 8: The Promise of God's Goodness

No good thing will be withheld from them that
walk uprightly.
—Psalm 84:11

Continuing the thought from yesterday's entry, the Lord has only good intentions toward us. He never thinks or perpetrates evil against us. Too often people ask, "Why did God cause this awful thing to happen to me?" when the truth is, God did not cause it to happen at all. This life is a life of woe and if God had His way in the beginning, it would not be this way.

Despite this, God still promises that in this world of woe, He will bring good to them who walk with Him. To be sure there are conditions before we can claim God's promises, but these are easily met.

In fact, not only are the conditions to all his promises easy, but they can all be satisfied at one time through one action, namely, the exercising of our faith. As a child we wished for things to be, but seldom saw our wishes come true. With God, our wishes or desires can all come true. They are powered by prayer and realized by faith. Trust is the evidence of faith. Trust is us expecting, even assuming something will be, merely because God said it would.

Exercise your faith today. God will not withhold from the up-right any good thing. Ask Him to help you with the sorrow and pain that has come from the passing of your beloved pet. Ask Him to confirm in your heart that your best friend lives on and is well. Ask Him to bring his peace to you, that peace that passes all understanding. And finally, ask Him to fill the void that has been left in your life.

Day 9: The Promise to Guide Us

Delight thyself in the Lord and he shall give you
the desires of thine heart.
—Psalm 37:4

When we read this verse, there is a tendency to think that it means whatever we desire God will give to us. Actually, in some ways that is true. The idea is supported by teachings in the New Testament as well as throughout the Psalms. For instance, the Lord said *"Ye have not because ye ask not."* In truth, if a believer asks something of the Lord, He is usually inclined to grant the request provided it is not lustful, against some principle found in His word, or harmful to us.

Still, this verse really is not speaking about our expressed de-sires to God, but rather the desires He will give to us if we de-light ourselves in Him. In other words, God promises that if we are enthusiastic about the relationship of trust we have with Him, He will furnish us with our desires. He will fill our hearts and minds with things of greater value than the things we think are important.

For example, you are probably wondering why your pet was allowed to pass. You might even be blaming God for allowing it to happen. Of course, He is not to blame. He is the giver and sustainer of life. Unfortunately, physical life ends for all living things on this earth and there are no variances from that rule.

The passing of our pet is a traumatic time, but our lives consist of more than just the relationship we have with our pets. If we delight ourselves in the Lord and have a thankful spirit for the many good years He gave to us and our pet, accepting our circumstances will become a bit easier. Moreover, He will be able to change our heart's desire in order to help us focus again on the purpose and plans of our lives.

Tomorrow we will learn how to personalize this.

Day 10: The Promise to Give Courage

What time I am afraid, I will trust in thee.
—Psalm 56:3

This Psalm addresses the mercy of God. The Psalmist learned from experience that when he was at his lowest, when his fears raged within, this was the time to trust most in God. The indication is clear. God will give peace and courage to those who trust in Him.

In times of distress, such as the loss of a precious pet, God will mercifully instill courage within our hearts to allow us to carry on. This is not just a pipe dream. God says He will do it, and remember, a promise made by God is a promise kept.

Yesterday, we learned that God will give the trusting heart new desires. When we are deep in grief, we can be fearful of what the future holds and our desire is to sometimes give up. God in His mercy replaces that desire with a desire to trust even more in Him, and the result of more trust is a persevering courage.

Experiencing the loss of a pet gives place to many fears. We can fear to face the future because we feel each day will be filled with grief. We can be afraid to go to work, because we don't want others to see us when we are most vulnerable. We can reject the idea of ever having another pet, because we are afraid of facing this pain again.

God does not identify any particular type of fear in our passage, so I am inclinded to believe that it addresses all fear. If we want to overcome our fears, the remedy is simply that we need to trust in the Lord. Trust that the days ahead will be better. Trust that our coworkers will give us such support that we will not feel vulnerable. Trust that if we allow our hearts to love another pet, that the many years of unconditional love and devotion will far outweigh any fear of the future.

Day 11: The Promise of Delivery

*Then they cried unto the Lord in their trouble and
he delivered them out of their distresses.*
—Psalm 107:6

When something is repeated in the Bible, it is not folly to think God was assigning special emphasis to the truth being addressed. Sometimes we need to hear something more than once in order for it to register. Any wife whose husband is routinely absorbed in a football game on television will attest to this.

In this Psalm, the words found in verse 6 are repeated again in verses 13, 19, and 28. With this amount of emphasis, certainly we are being taught a valuable truth about trust. The message is that when your trust causes you to turn to the Lord, He rewards your faith by delivering you.

The important thing to note here is that this verse is not necessarily speaking of military campaigns or natural disasters, but simply the stresses of everyday life. As we will see in more detail in our next daily devotion, God is a very present help. He is eager to help in our daily lives in any way we allow him to.

Are you still trying to deal with your grief and sorrow on your own? Are you still wondering why the Lord would allow your precious best friend to pass? Why not give these things over to someone who is able to deliver you from them? Remember, it isn't that your pet isn't precious to God; it is just that you are more precious. Your pet is safe in his care. It is you He is concerned about now.

Please go back to this Psalm and read verse 43. Here is a promise that can be yours if you are wise enough to ask for it.

Day 12: The Promise to Help

God is our refuge and strength, a very present help
in trouble.
—Psalm 46:1

This is a very potent promise. It does not say God can help. It does not say that God might help. It doesn't even say that He will help. It says He is a present help, or that He is currently helping.

When you couple this thought with the truth expounded by the Lord in the gospels where he told us *"My Father knows what things you have need of,"* it has huge implications. Essentially, God promises foreknowledge of a need and instantaneous help to meet that need. In other words, He is helping before we even know we need help.

This transposes well to the needs of people who love pets when the time comes to bid farewell. Their passing may catch us by surprise, but God is never caught off guard. He knew the day of their passing just as He knows the day of our own passing. Anticipating our need for His comfort and help, He addressed the concerns we would have in his word, which, coincidentally, are captured in this book.

He has indeed provided help for our present need. Find comfort in this thought and cast your cares upon him for He knew you would need His help and has an unlimited reservoir available to you.

Day 13: The Promise to Make Things Right

And God shall wipe away all tears from their eyes;
and there shall be no more death, neither
sorrow, nor crying.
—Revelation 21:4

Embodied in this scripture are many of the promises and hopes that comprise our faith. Perhaps this is why it is one of this writer's favorite passages.

Of all the promises, this is one of the sweetest, that death, sorrow, and pain are living on borrowed time. Their days are numbered. These have been the dreaded enemies of humanity. These have individually and collectively made this world a world of woe. Their presence and impact will not be missed.

Until that day we have to cope, but God makes that coping tolerable and manageable through the myriad promises He offers to us by faith. One grand day we will witness the long awaited passing of these enemies. Until then, let us continuously meditate on the other promises that are available for today and find real comfort in them.

Your tears for your pet are tears of love. Tears are a language known to all people, but appreciated most by the creator. He knows the pain you feel and the anguish of not being able to change the circumstances of your life. But He wants you to know that He is aware, He is watching and helping, and one day He shall wipe away all tears from your eyes. Let this promise strengthen you as you face this day.

Day 14: The Promise of Reward

And let us not be weary in well doing, for in due season we shall reap.
—Galatians 6:9

Allow me to take this verse out of context a bit so that I might apply the principle being taught in a way relevant to you and your loss. My application might seem a bit abstract, but I think there are many ways to use a verse in a positive way apart from its primary purpose without being heretical.

It has been at least two weeks now since your pet passed. I know the idea of getting another pet so soon is something many people do not like to consider. You may be one of them, but please hear me out before you dismiss the idea.

Some consider another pet a replacement and therefore a betrayal of the pet that has departed. I can understand this, but it does not have to be framed in such a way. A part of my heart will always belong to my departed best friends and no other pet will be allowed to infringe upon their space. However, I have room in my heart for others. I have room to honor my departed pet by rescuing one of her kind from a shelter and perhaps certain death.

There are so many that wait for the door of the shelter to open and for someone to point them out and say, "That one, that is the one I want." Think of the good this would do to your heart, to be the hero of an animal in such need. In no time, this animal would focus its devotion and love toward you and your heart would find new reason to love again. Love is a good neutralizer of sorrow.

The bottom line is that this would be "well doing" on your part and the reward would be a heart on the mend.

Day 15: The Promise to Never Leave You

I will not leave you comfortless.
—John 14:18

No doubt these words were spoken by the Lord to signal the coming of the Comforter or Holy Spirit. The comfort he was to provide was to assure believers that the Lord had not left without intention of returning for them. It would be difficult for me to apply this verse to our topic of pet loss without pointing out that comfort in other areas of our lives is secondary to that.

Nevertheless, comfort is available. When you end your day in tears of sorrow and awake the next morning to find your pain is still with you, it is hard to imagine that anyone or anything could bring the comfort you seek, but God's promises are true. He said He would not leave us comfortless.

God wants to deliver His comfort to us, but the onus is on us to accept it and put it into action. The way we do this is to pray and ask Him for it. But this is not the end of our responsibility.

The Bible tells us to ask with nothing wavering. Again, it boils down to faith and faith only comes from trust.

Today, refortify your faith. Take God at His word and believe it is true. Believe He says what He means and that His promises are kept.

Day 16: The Promise to Heal

He healeth the broken in heart, and bindeth up
their wounds.
—**Psalm 147:3**

It may be difficult to picture God in this role of Army Field Nurse, but He says that He will bind up our wounds and heal our broken hearts. Of course we understand that He is speaking of wounds of the heart and not exterior wounds; but in any event, it is God who nurses us.

The loss of a pet can often break the heart in more pieces than other sorrows. On top of this, friends and family can fail you in your hour of need by saying cruel or callous things, exacerbating your pain but fear not, for in the midst of your calamity, God will bring spiritual bandages to bind up your emotional wounds. Not only does He give us promise that our animals live on, which gives us comfort for today, but He assures there can be a reunion, which gives hope for the future.

You have passed the halfway point in our devotionals. I hope you have disciplined yourself to have read only one entry each day to maximize the impact over a period of time. If you read them all at once you will circumvent the intended use, much like antibiotics, which must be taken in regimen to effect a cure.

I hope, too, that by now the promises of God have given you renewed hope and purpose. There is power in the things God has uttered, but only when we accept them by faith.

We will meet again tomorrow.

Day 17: The Promise to Be with Us

Teaching them to observe all things . . . and lo,
I am with you always.
—Matthew 28:20

What a comfort it is to know that God promises to be with us always. Think about the implications. Throughout the ages God has been present. There has not been a time when He was not minding His creation. Presidents have passed; judges and policemen have passed; clergy, too; but God lives on.

God also is omniscient. He has all knowledge. There is nothing to know that He does not already know. No one can inform Him about something and nothing can occur to Him. He is aware of everything that is happening everywhere in the world and universe. Nothing escapes His watchful eye.

He boils this authority and power down to a personal level and encourages us by saying, *"Lo, I am with you always."* Among nearly 7 billion people, we stand out to God. At the same time, He singles out and cares about the other 7 billion at the same time. What amazing power God has!

You miss your pet. God is aware of that. Your heart is broken. He knows. As you work through your pain, He is aware of that, too. As you seek to return to normal in your life, He makes His power available to help. Whether you call upon Him to help or not is up to you, but He will remain available in case you do.

Day 18: The Promise to Give Life

> *He that believeth on the Son hath everlasting life.*
> —John 3:36

The most precious promise we have of God is that of regeneration. By the simple act of believing in Him we are made new and given unending life. We absolutely do not merit this consideration and we are not able to earn it. It is something God simply promises to those who believe.

For our precious pets, and for all His animals, this promise does not apply. Don't let that bother you. It does not apply, because there is no need for it to. Animals enjoy the same innocence they have always enjoyed since the garden. Their status with God has never changed and they remain "safe" in his providence.

If this truth has not yet grabbed you and filled you with joy, perhaps it is time it did. I know that your heart aches for your departed best friend. I know how difficult it has been for you to cope with this traumatic change in your life. But sometimes, when we truly love, as you do, we can temporarily set aside our own unhappiness and experience real joy for the good fortune that has befallen the one we love.

Too often we view death from this side only. From our perspective, it appears dark, mysterious, and forbidding. We see it as an unwanted ending. There is another view, however. From the other side, death is not dark or mysterious. It is a beginning. It is the start of a life in a place of wonder and splendor.

Today's promise is for you and me. Our pets have already received the promise without condition. Comfort yourself with this truth—your best friend is alive, well, and happy.

Day 19: The Promise to Stand with Us

The Lord is my shepherd, I shall not want.
—Psalm 23:1

What a claim for someone to be able to make . . . that the Lord is *my* shepherd. How utterly personal the Lord makes His commitment to us. It should thrill you to know that you are that important to Him.

This verse, coupled with the other five that comprise the twenty-third Psalm, are reportedly the most familiar passages in the Bible and also the most commonly quoted. Over the centuries, this Psalm has comforted the hearts of millions, from children saying their bedtime prayers to those grieving the passing of a cherished loved one or pet. These powerful words have turned sorrow into victory, saved and changed countless lives, and even swayed the course of history.

Of the 119 words that make up this Psalm, more than 80 percent are simple one-syllable words. The rest are two-or-more-syllable words, none of which are complex in meaning or application. That God could accomplish such greatness with the simple words of this Psalm is a testament to His ability to be the Great Shepherd.

A shepherd watches over his flock and knows each of his sheep. With him they never want or fear. During the time that you grieve the passing of your pet, please be aware that you are like a pet to the Lord. He is the shepherd and we the sheep. He knows His sheep and what they are going through and like a good shepherd, He will go with you every step of the way.

Day 20: The Promise of Freedom

And ye shall know the truth and the truth shall set
you free.
—John 8:32

For the purpose of our devotional study, this truth that sets us free from our sorrow is the knowledge that the Lord is not just the Lord of life, but also over death.

It might shock you to learn that physical death is never a permanent state. Some people claim it is, but they cannot find any support for their view in scripture. Their position is based solely and wholly on their opinion and it is anyone's guess what that is based upon. Essentially, God does not agree with them and their opinion does not carry any weight.

The fact is that death is a very brief experience in time. It is the intermediate state that affects passage from this life to the next. We are not discussing people now or we would have much more to talk about. We are discussing our pets and other animals and God's providential care for them.

Like humans, death is the natural conclusion of life for animals. It is the conduit they must pass through in order to enter the next life. It would be wonderful if there was a plane or ship they (and we) could board to make that journey, but the only method of transport available to us at the moment is death.

Since the Lord has power and authority over death, we can safely assume that what He says about it is true. In effect, death is brief, extremely brief. We pass from life unto life, briefly passing through death. Knowing this truth should set you free from the dark imaginations of your mind and give you peace concerning the passing of your pet.

Day 21: The Promise That He Will Answer Us

Call unto me and I will answer thee.
—Jeremiah 33:3

Could you pick up the telephone and call the president of the United States? You could place a call, but the person who answers it will undoubtedly be an administrative assistant or clerk. It is not realistic to think that you would be able to speak with the Chief Executive without an appointment.

You could write a letter, but again, the likelihood of it reaching the president and him taking the time to read it is extremely low. No doubt you will receive a response that appears to be signed by him and it will read as if he were personally answering you. In reality, it will be a canned response with a facsimile signature affixed by machine and nothing more.

This should not be of too much concern to you as it is an expected result. The president is much too busy to respond to each of the many thousands of letters and e-mails that are sent to him each week. Besides, politicians long ago left off being concerned about individuals and now focus on polls. None, especially the president, can afford precious time for us personally.

This only serves to make our verse that much more special. God runs the whole universe and yet there is nothing more important to Him than you and me. He always has time to hear and to respond. In fact, He publishes his telephone number for public consumption. When you call J333, you won't get any administrative assistants or clerks. The Lord Himself answers all incoming calls.

The promises of God are sweet and true. I would encourage you to spend more time calling His personal number and speaking to Him about the way you feel. He understands grief and has a balm for it. He understand tears and is able to dry them permanently.

Day 22: The Promise of Joy

*Weeping may endure for a night, but joy cometh
in the morning.*
—Psalm 30:5

The promise of joy to the faithful is another of the sweeter promises God makes to us. We have the assurance that though sorrows will come, they will always eventually give way to joy.

Many confuse the word *joy* with *happiness*. In fact, the two words are completely different in meaning. Happiness is reactive. It is conditional and temporal. Circumstances in our lives can give us happiness or rob us of it. At best, happiness is fleeting.

Not so joy. Joy is something we have because of our faith. It is not reactive or fleeting, but rather constant and lasting. It is essentially the state of mind created by faith. By another name we might call it assurance.

Today, you may not be happy because of the passing of your beloved pet. You truly have a reason to be unhappy. But your faith-based joy should lift you above your pain and allow you to bask in the promises of God that sorrow is of short duration and that He is in control.

Day 23: The Promise of Victory

In all things we are more than conquerors.
—Romans 8:37

To be a conqueror is not enough for those of faith. We are to be more than conquerors. Conquerors are those who defeat and overthrow. They themselves can be conquered if their adversaries are strong enough. Not so the faithful. Our hope and trust is in one who is able every time, all the time. In faith there can be no defeat. In faith there can only be victory.

I am sure that your pain is still a significant factor in your life. It will take some time to conquer the sense of loss and grief. If you look back on the previous three weeks, however, I think you will find that you have made substantial progress. At the very least, we have discussed issues that should settle in your mind that your best friend remains alive and well. This knowledge alone should take much of the burden away.

As we near a close to these thirty days of trying to understand how the promises of God apply to our lives and situations, I hope you will continue to glean gems from the remaining entries. While I have asked that you not look ahead in these lessons, it would be quite all right for you to go back and review. Reminding yourself of the great things that are available to you can only serve to encourage.

Day 24: The Promise of Strength

But they that wait upon the Lord shall renew
their strength . . . they shall mount up with
wings like eagles.
—Isaiah 40:31

You have been waiting on the Lord and trusting him to help in this great time of need. He is faithful and will bring to fruition that which He has promised, if He hasn't already done so.

It is not by chance that the Lord likens those of faith to eagles. Ever the symbol of strength and victory, these noble creatures represent the persevering spirit that those of faith should project. In previous verses of this section of scripture, we are guaranteed victory when we trust in his strength. In one verse we are told that *"He gives power to the faint."*

Undoubtedly there have been times since your loss that you have felt faint, or too weak to carry on. Your own strength was just not enough. One day you are able to cope and the next you are again in despair. It is normal to not be normal at times like these.

Unfortunately, if you are relying on your own strength to see you through, you will experience many bad or undesirable days. In our verse we are encouraged to wait on or seek the Lord's strength. When we do, He renews us, or makes us right again. And that after all, is our goal, to be right again.

You can and must mount up over your grief and sorrow. I know that you miss your best friend. I have been there many,

many times. Life's blows can hurt, but they cannot stop the one who has God's promise of strength.

Day 25: The Promise That We Will Persevere

A thousand shall fall at thy side and ten thousand
at thy right hand, but it shall not come nigh thee.
—Psalm 91:7

Use of this verse in the context I am going to use it may seem a bit strange, but I think it fits quite well.

The children of Israel relied on the promises of God as they sought to occupy the land that God had given them. They were told of the calamity that would be all around them, but rested on the promise that it would not come near them. The only times that Israel suffered were when they allowed their faith to waver. When their faith was strong, they persevered.

I encourage you to exercise your faith to make it stronger each day. No one is saying that you do not have a right to hurt. No one is saying that losing a pet is easy. What I am saying is that you have learned how to apply faith over your grief and seen the positive results. Now, apply it to every aspect of your life and benefit from the promises you have learned.

A few weeks ago, you were ready to give up. Where thousands had fallen before, you were in danger of falling. But you have the promise that it will not come near unto you if you apply your faith and trust that God will get you through it all.

Day 26: The Promise of Peace

*Thou wilt keep him in perfect peace whose mind is
stayed on thee.*
—Isaiah 26:3

Another scripture that compliments today's thought is found in the book of John. In this passage, the Lord says *"Peace I give you, not as the world giveth."*

The world is represented by our elected government. Our government gives us a certain amount of peace in our lives. We enjoy safety from foreign enemies through our military. We have reasonable safety in our communities because of government law enforcement. There are utilities and services that make our lives easier and bring us peace of mind. It is comforting to know that the hardships we might otherwise face ourselves are taken care of by our government.

Still, this peace is not on the level of the peace that the Lord offers to us. His peace is one that transcends this life and its woes. It is an eternal and complete peace. In fact, our scripture labels it as "perfect" peace.

As you near the end of our devotional series, I hope you have come to recognize that delivery from your sorrow can only truly be realized by having the peace of God. Don't concentrate on your problems and the things that so easily beset you. Stay your mind rather on the one who can give you perfect peace. The one you miss so much is safe in His hands and that alone should bring you great joy and peace.

Day 27: The Promise of Cheer

Be of good cheer, I have overcome the world.
—John 16:33

In previous entries we looked at conquering our sorrow, renewing our strength, achieving the victory, and a host of other important topics. Today we see how it is that all these things have been made available to us. The Lord accomplished it. He faced the woes of this world and tells us to be of good cheer, that he overcame the world.

What must we do to be cheerful? There are no prerequisites given. There are no conditions we must meet. The only thing we are tasked with is to do it. Be cheerful. In essence we are being told that the world is no longer a problem because Jesus has defeated it. Death is no longer a threat to those of faith, because he defeated it. Innocents like children and animals have no worries about death either for they are "safe" in his care. It seems there is good reason to have great cheer.

There is no trick to being cheerful. There is no secret handshake or special PIN number you have to enter. It only requires that you be cheerful. This is what faith is. You don't see it. You can't point it out. It just is taking God at his word and acting upon it. The Lord said "be of good cheer" and that is all we need to have cheer.

While there is much for your heart to lament, you are now aware that there is much more to rejoice over. Be of good cheer. It is time for you to smile again.

Day 28: The Promise of Power

But God has not given us the spirit of fear, but of
power and a sound mind.
—2 Timothy 1:7

Often, the passing of a loved one be they human or animal, shakes us to our very core. We wonder why life is so cruel and why we have no control over the things that befall us. It is easy at times like these to be afraid and uncertain. It is easy to feel alone.

Our scripture reminds us that the spirit of fear is not from God and we should not yield to it. He has given us the spirit of power. It is not the kind of power that we can misuse for selfish gain, but that will help us persevere over our own emotions and apprehensions. This power comes from on high and is crafted to help us win the battle that goes on inside of our hearts and minds.

This is where we enjoy the spirit of a sound mind. We should not subject ourselves any longer to the tortures of despair and grief. We know He is true. We know His promises are true and that all the ill that has befallen us will be made right one day.

Through the course of these devotionals you have learned much about persevering and overcoming. It is time to put to use all the things you have learned and purpose in your heart to be happy again. Of course you can continue to grieve your wonderful pet, but do so in context. That context would be that you had no control over their passing, it was a passing on and not a passing away and that you can see them again.

Day 29: The Promise of a Wise Plan

All things work together for good to them that love
God.
—Romans 8:28

The condition to this promise will cause many to fall short of claiming it. Some have difficulty with proclaiming a love for God. Again, God keeps it simple for people like this writer. What scripture teaches is that to love God we merely need to believe in Him and trust Him.

This means we need to believe all that He says. To that end, we have looked at thirty promises that He has made, or at least we will have with tomorrow's entry . . . and to enjoy these promises, we need only to believe.

Again, your experience of losing a pet has been extremely traumatic. I understand this, but I believe God understands it more perfectly. When He had the words of this verse penned, I think He knew that a wide scope of applications would be used under the umbrella of this promise by people of all ages.

Today, I submit to you that while you have sorrowed and grieved over your loss, God says that He will turn this experience into something good, perhaps even great. I admit that you may not readily recognize the good as it occurs, but you can rest assured that good will come from this life's experience. It is my hope that a closer relationship with the Lord and the benefits that go with that will be one of those good things.

Whatever and whenever the Lord performs this good, I hope

you will think back and be able to validate that God drew something good from your suffering, that He did not forget you and was always in control.

Day 30: The Promise of Blessings

Surely goodness and mercy will follow me all the
days of my life.
—Psalm 23:6

I could not leave a series on God's promises with only one reference to the twenty-third Psalm, because it has meant so much to so many for so long. The Bible is timeless, and yet timely. These 119 words have been embraced by people of every land, in every walk of life, throughout history.

In these few words we find the promise of blessings that a Jewish rabbi found twenty centuries ago or that a Brazilian farmer found a thousand years later. They mean as much today to us as they did to them then. They hold as much power.

Life can bring trials and distress to anyone, and usually does at some point in one's life. Kings are not exempt. Paupers do not get a pass. Life on this earth can be wonderful, but fickle. One moment we can be on top of the world, and the next we can be undone and at wit's end. Your attention to this devotional is proof of just how bad life can treat us at times for you have endured a painful passing.

Now that I have stated the obvious, I hope that it is also evident that the solution to a calamitous life is to place one's faith in the Lord. Here the Psalmist, who struggled with great grief and distress in his own life, claims a promise that is available to each of us today. He knew by faith that God was to bless the remainder of his life.

The invitation to this promise is open to all. It is my hope that you will claim it for yourself. May God richly bless you.